KB063109

2010 JPI PeaceNet Series

Dialogue for Peace and Cooperation in East Asia

Jeju Peace Institute Research Series ⑭

2010 JPI PeaceNet Series
Dialogue for Peace and Cooperation in East Asia

Edited by Jeju Peace Institute

ORUEM Publishing House

Jeju Peace Institute Research Series ⑭

2010 JPI PeaceNet Series

Dialogue for Peace and Cooperation in East Asia

Edited by Jeju Peace Institute

Jeju Peace Institute
2572 Jungmun-dong, Seogwipo City
Jeju Special Self-Governing Province, 697-120, Korea
Tel: +82-64-735-6500   Fax: +82-64-735-6512
E-mail: jejupeace@jpi.or.kr   http://www.jpi.or.kr

Published by ORUEM Publishing House
1420-6 Seocho 1-dong, Seocho-gu, Seoul, Korea
TEL: +82-2-585-9122~3
E-mail: oruem@oruem.co.kr

ISBN 978-89-7778-351-5   03300

Preface

On the Occasion of the Publication of a Book Containing Articles Published Via the JPI PeaceNet in 2010

In connection with its efforts to promote peace and collaboration in East Asia, the Jeju Peace Institute created the JPI PeaceNet as a forum through which neighboring countries could express their opinions on a variety of subjects and exchange with each other, in 2010 as well as in the preceding year. Sadly, the international community's efforts to resolve the problem caused by North Korea's nuclear program have stalled, while the provocative acts perpetrated by the North in 2010 including the attack on the ROKS Cheonan and the shelling of Yeonpyeongdo Island continue to pose a direct threat to the security of the Korean Peninsula. Regional peace in East Asia is also threatened by the ongoing territorial disputes between China and Japan over the

Senkaku Islands (Diaoyudao) and between Japan and Russia over the Northern Territories. Furthermore, the issues surrounding China's human rights record and the struggle for democratization, which reemerged on the occasion of Liu Xiaobo's having received the Nobel Peace Prize, appear to have ignited a new ideological confrontation in East Asia.

This year, the JPI PeaceNet has gone a long way in its efforts to promote peace in the region, serving as an arena for the expression of a variety of views and the exchange of ideas. Scholars, experts, journalists, and ordinary people have provided plenty of support in connection with the publication of articles over the Internet.

It is nice to see the precious articles contributed to the JPI PeaceNet now being published in the form of a book. I would like to express my heartfelt gratitude to the contributors of the articles and to the members of staff at the Institute who dedicated so much time and energy to this project. Thanks are also due to President Boo Seong-Ok of Oruem Publishing House for his cooperation in the publication of relevant research materials. I also owe a great debt to all those who have encouraged us and given us invaluable advice.

December 2010

President of Jeju Peace Institute

HAN Tae-kyu

Contents

Preface • 5

Part 2   Multilateral Cooperation in East Asia

Part 3 Denuclearization in East Asia

Part 4

Global Issue
and the Human Rights

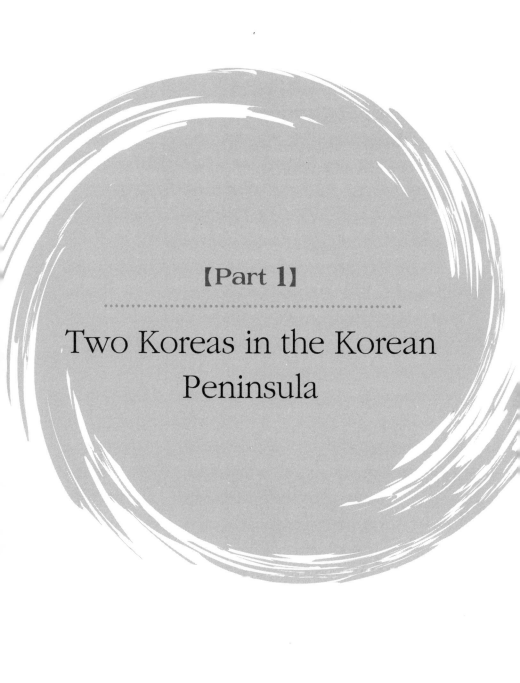

【Part 1】

Two Koreas in the Korean Peninsula

The Cheonan Sinking and ROK-U.S. Cooperation

KIM Hyun-Wook
Institute of Foreign Affairs and National Security

Two months have passed since North Korea's attack on the ROKS Cheonan. The relations between the two Koreas are rapidly deteriorating, following the South Korean government's announcement of the result of the investigation of the incident on May 20. Neighboring countries appear to be busy considering what countermeasure they should take.

▌Three Main Reasons for North Korea's Attack on the Cheonan

We can think of the following reasons for North Korea's attack:

First, reprisal for the Daecheong Sea Battle of 10th November 2009. One of North Korea's patrol boats was severely damaged and ran away from the scene of the battle. In February 2010, North Korea held a rally calling for reprisal against South Korea.

Second, North Korea's internal situation. At present, North Korea has some main problems to solve: Kim Jong-il's poor health; power transfer; and the aggravating economic situation. It is possible that the North perpetrated the incident to build an internal solidarity in connection with such problems.

Finally, a card concerning the Six-Party Talks. North Korea and the U.S. were in negotiation for North Korea's return to the Six-Party Talks right before the occurrence of the Cheonan incident. Historically, North Korea has taken a strategy of coming to the negotiation table and simultaneously showing a hard-line attitude. It perpetrated the Rangoon terror incident in Myanmar in 1983 amidst the negotiation for the tripartite meeting with the South and the U.S. It is not unusual for North Korea to take an abruptly unexpected action to slow down the process of negotiation and make the situation develop in a way favorable to it or to diversify agenda items at a negotiation and change the negotiation framework. The Cheonan incident also appears to have something to do with its intention to slow down the conditions favorable to it.

At Present, the ROK and the U.S. Maintain Relations of Close Cooperation Concerning the Cheonan Incident. Details of the Bilateral Collaboration Can be Summarized as Follows:

First, the two countries are discussing a plan to refer the case to the UN Security Council. Korean vice Foreign Minister Chon Young-woo paid a visit to the U.S. Deputy Secretary James B. Steinberg and discussed when and how the matter should be referred to the UN Security Council. It is likely that the UN Security Council will end in the adoption of its President's statement on the case due to China backing North Korea's position. The ROK and the U.S. will continue to discuss the matter after the UN Security Council takes a stance.

Second, the U.S. decided to provide the technology (i.e. undersea sonar scanner or AWACS-related technology) for tracking enemy submersibles to the ROK to help it supplement its capability in relevant naval operations.

Third, the two countries are planning to carry out training exercises against North Korea's submarines in the West Sea, and the exercises will include the participation of a 97,000-ton class, nuclear-powered aircraft carrier, the USS George Washington, aegis class cruisers, 7 or 8 destroyers, and some nuclear-powered submarines under the control of the U.S. Navy 7th Fleet. It is expected that the exercises will deliver a strong message to North Korea and China.

Finally, the two countries are discussing the need to postpone the planned transfer of the wartime operational control. The current U.S. security policy stresses the concept of strategic flexibility and includes the return of wartime operational control to the ROK. Still, it knows that the current security situation of the ROK requires reconsideration of the return of the control, which was originally scheduled for 2012.

❙ Several Factors of the ROK-U.S. Collaboration are Different from Those During the Bush Administration

First, the Joint Vision for the Alliance of the ROK and the U.S. adopted in June 2009 puts the core of the bilateral alliance on joint values and the establishment of mutual trust. That means efforts made to develop the alliance which used to focus on the strategic interests of each country have gone into deepened relations of alliance. The two countries have worked in close cooperation based on the joint vision in the wake of the Cheonan incident.

Second, the ROK used to be the beneficiary of the one-sided

security-related aid from the U.S., but the newly established bilateral alliance asks for a more balanced collaboration between the two countries in broader regions of the world, including the entire East Asia, as in the ROK's dispatch of troops to Afghanistan or the two countries' close cooperation following the Cheonan incident.

Third, the Bush Administration used to adopt a unilateral defense/ diplomacy policy, but the new U.S. Administration under the leadership of Barack Obama stresses alliance relations with other countries and the role of international organizations as highlighted in the Quadrennial Defense Review (QDR) and NSS (National Security Strategy) reports. The new stance taken by the U.S. appears to contribute to the reinforcement of the alliance relations between the ROK and the U.S.

At present, the ROK and the U.S. take a hardline stance against North Korea, but China appears to be unwilling to collaborate with them as a country that can exert influence on North Korea. China still maintains a cold-war way of thinking about the situation on the Korean Peninsula. In its policy concerning the Korean Peninsula, the priority is stability. China appears to put the stability of the Korean Peninsula before the efforts for denuclearization of North Korea, while the main purpose of the Six-Party Talks is the management of the situation on the Korean

Peninsula through denuclearization of North Korea. Concerning the Cheonan incident, the Chinese government reiterates the principle it has adopted for the Korean Peninsula—its opposition to any attempt to cause a conflict. It shows that it is not easy to expect China to join in the stance jointly adopted by the ROK and the U.S.

China insists that the Six-Party Talks be held simultaneously with the efforts made concerning the Cheonan incident, but the joint stance adopted by the ROK and the U.S. is that the Cheonan incident should be settled before the resumption of the Six-Party Talks. Some U.S. experts already view the Six-Party Talks as a failure. The possibility of the denuclearization of North Korea appears to be slim even if North Korea returns to the Six-Party Talks. The thing is that North Korea's return to the Six-Party Talks is meaningless. What is important is not the choice between the settlement of the Cheonan incident and the resumption of the Six-Party Talks, especially when China's priority concerning its policy about the Korean Peninsula is not denuclearization of North Korea.

▌ Measures to Be Taken by the ROK and the U.S.

First, their policy concerning China. At present, the bilateral policy collaboration between the ROK and the U.S. is swayed by the China factor. Even the UN Security Council-initiated sanctions against North Korea are likely to be replaced by its President's statement due to the intervention of China. Without China's cooperation, the international community's sanctions against North Korea will not go far. The process of the denuclearization of North Korea also depends on the attitude taken by China. China regards North Korea as an important buffer zone. The collapse of North Korea's current regime will result in China's bordering the ROK in which US Forces are stationed. China will never want such a situation. Under the current circumstances, it is necessary for the ROK and the U.S. to deliver their hardline commitment against North Korea concerning the responsibility of the Cheonan incident, making it clear that the stability on the Korean Peninsula cannot be attained without China's collaboration. Simultaneously, the ROK should make efforts to help China put an end to its cold-war way of thinking, while building efforts for invigoration of economic exchange with China as through an FTA with it.

Second, policy collaboration between the ROK and the U.S. The Cheonan incident makes it necessary to consider a change in the combined defense stance between the two countries. In its QDR released this year, the U.S. presented the need for a flexible security policy in preparation against various and unspecified security threats. The two countries should establish a combined defense stance against various security threats, including the military threats of North Korea, based on such a flexible policy. In its recently released NPR (Nuclear Posture Review), the U.S. disclosed a plan to promote its extended nuclear deterrence with conventional combat strength and a MD (missile defense) system, in addition to existing nuclear weapons. The two countries should continue to make efforts for promotion of such diverse combat strength. It is also necessary to push ahead with a "soft power" policy toward North Korea, as the Obama Administration has done toward people of Afghanistan and Iraq so that they may feel friendly toward the U.S. Currently, it appears that agitation among the people poses a serious threat to North Korea's regime. The ROK and the U.S. need to consider adopting a new policy concerning North Korea with such a situation taken into account.

Finally, the importance of the tripartite security-related collaboration between the ROK, the U.S. and Japan. The role of the ROK appears to be particularly important in connection with the need for the tripartite collaboration due to the alienation of the relations between the U.S. and Japan. The ROK needs to strive to reinvigorate the role of the ROK-U.S.-Japan Trilateral Coordination and Oversight Group (TCOG) on the occasion of the Cheonan incident.

---

* JPI PeaceNet No.14 published on June 8, 2010 in Korean

North Korea Policy after the UNSC Presidential Statement on the Sinking of the Cheonan

RHEE Bong-Jo
Former Vice Unification Minister

On July 9, 2010, the UN Security Council adopted a presidential statement on the sinking of the South Korean corvette, the Cheonan, three and a half months after the incident (which occurred in March), and 35 days after the referral of the case to the UNSC. The UN's action concerning the incident was concluded, although the permanent member countries of the UNSC were divided in their views about the incident, and the contents of the statement remain controversial. Furthermore, the incident was not settled with the issuance of the UNSC statement

The tragic incident can be traced back to the recent heightening of tension and confrontation between the two Koreas that aggravated the security situation particularly along the Northern Limit Line (NLL). The incident is ultimately a case that should be settled between the two Koreas. From the beginning, it was difficult to expect the UNSC to take clear-cut and binding measures concerning the incident. As it happens, the direction of bilateral relations between the two Koreas in the aftermath of the incident will be delineated by how the South intends to settle the incident. In the statement made to the South Koreans on May 24, South Korean President Lee Myung-bak asked the North to apologize for the attack and to punish those responsible. However, it is doubtful whether the North will accommodate such a request, as the North has asserted that the incident was a "sheer fabrication" concocted by the South. Such doubt is strengthened further by the uneven attitude in favor of the North shown by China and Russia, and by the tone of the statement contained in the UNSC President's statement.

Essentially, the incident is a matter that should be settled between the two Koreas, and how they settle it will remain a matter of crucial interest. However, it is unrealistic to deal with the incident within the current inter-Korea dialogue framework, as mutual trust has been exhausted due to the seriousness of the incident. It appears that the South Korean government did not intend to handle the case as an inter-Korean issue at the beginning, perhaps based on such a judgment. The referral of the matter to the UNSC was the expected course of action, but the countries concerned started showing different attitudes with the passing of time, according to their national interests. The various countries of Northeast Asia have different views of the incident, depending on their national interests. Under such circumstances, inter-Korea relations will inevitably go through a long, dark tunnel. Granted, it will not be wise to sit down with arms folded. It is necessary to do something.

The UNSC statement issued on July 9 calls for full adherence to the Korean Armistice Agreement and encourages the settlement of outstanding issues on the Korean peninsula by peaceful means, via a resumption of direct dialogue and negotiation through the appropriate channels as soon as possible, with a view to avoiding conflicts and averting escalation. The resumption of the Six-Party Talks concerning the North's nuclear program is another matter that should not be ignored indefinitely. It is feared that the North's nuclear capability will be further strengthened, with no substantial control imposed with the passage of time. Reactivation of the process concerning the Six-Party Talks may provide an appropriate opportunity to deal with the two pending issues. A direction for the settlement of the sinking of the Cheonan issue was proposed in the UNSC statement after a process of discussion between the relevant countries; the Six-Party Talks may provide an opportunity to discuss how to adhere to the Armistice Agreement and prevent clashes between the two Koreas in accordance with the UNSC recommendation, in addition to efforts made to settle the issue of the North's nuclear program. If some progress is made at the Six-Party Talks, the two Koreas should be able to handle the Cheonan incident as the directly related parties.

The North may feel relieved by the UNSC statement, which did not pinpoint it as the aggressor in the Cheonan incident or ask for additional sanctions against the North. The lenient nature of the statement may give the North a good excuse to re-join the Six-Party Talks. Following the UNSC statement, the North's Foreign Ministry spokesman said, "[We] will make consistent efforts to conclude a peace treaty and consider denuclearization on the basis of Six-Party Talks conducted on an equal footing," and the North is taking a positive attitude concerning dialogue with the UN Command at Panmunjom. It should be possible to find a way out of the current deadlocked situation without much difficulty. The U.S. and China will be able to operate the pre-Cheonan system of collaboration; although the North may set other preconditions for its re-joining the Six-Party Talks. It is possible to predict that the North will take a positive stance in its re-joining the Six-Party Talks based on the following premises.

First, the country feels that the survival of the regime has become a more pressing issue than it was at the time of the Joint Statement of the fourth round of the Six-Party Talks in Beijing, held on

September 19, 2005. Its demand for the withdrawal of the worldwide sanctions imposed against it and the discussions about a peace treaty conducted on a continual basis since earlier this year may ultimately be viewed as an attempt to find an excuse to return to the Six-Party Talks. This is something that North Korea had said it would never return to and there may be a request for the international community to provide economic support and a guarantee for the safety of the regime.

Second, for the forthcoming rounds of the Six-Party Talks, China will have to take on the South Korean government's former role of coordinator or promoter, and the North should consider this China's position. Third, the North will try to mitigate the South's offensive concerning the Cheonan incident by internationalizing the Korean Peninsula issue, while trying to further develop its relations with China and to improve its relations with the U.S. As a result, the Cheonan incident may deepen the Kim Jung-il regime's dependence on China. It may also end up putting a limit on the South's influence on the North by invalidating the Lee Myung-bak Administration's efforts to cause a fundamental change in the North. This is why the South should consider the need for a resumption of the Six-Party Talks before it is too late.

In the period following the UNSC's July 9 statement, any desirable course of action taken by the South concerning the North should include the establishment of a comprehensive and multi-faceted policy, while paying greater attention to the need for effective management of the situation. The South Korean government needs to take a cool-headed stance, appraising changes in the international situation in the wake of the Cheonan incident, and review its policy toward the North. It should remember that unless it is in the driver's seat and equipped with appropriate strategies, the U.S. and China will take the initiative. The South is in a more advantageous position than the North within the international community and the South should lead the way in finding a means to overcome the currently stalled situation. Squeezing the North alone cannot solve the problems involving the country. The series of punitive measures against the North announced by the South on May 24 can hardly bring about the desired results, with most of the leverage held by the South against the North exhausted. The South committed the folly of disclosing all the measures it could take against the North at the same time. The South's referral of the Cheonan case to the UNSC while laying the blame on the North met a series of insurmountable stumbling blocks. The contents of the UNSC statement fell some way short of what the South had expected in line with the punitive measures it took on May 24.

Given the previously mentioned circumstances, the South needs to consider an exit strategy based on "direct dialogue and negotiation through the appropriate channels" as recommended by the UNSC statement, with the aim of reestablishing its policy on the North, although it is not an alternative that the South can take immediately. To that end, the South should take the following steps: First, it should consider a policy shift, i.e. making an approach to the North Korean issue within a grander framework and through a perspective focusing on Northeast Asia rather than on the North alone. Second, it should actively take part in the Six-Party Talks, suggest alternatives intended to make it a more productive process of dialogue, and fine-tune the policies adopted with the aim of using the progress made in the Six-Party Talks as leverage for the normalization of relations with the North. Third, it should reinforce its collaboration with China so that China can exert greater influence on the North with regard to its taking more positive steps toward the goal of denuclearizing the Korean Peninsula, along with efforts to ease the level of distrust formed between the two countries due to the Cheonan incident and to secure progress in the Six-Party Talks. Fourth, it should strive to ease tensions and prevent clashes along the NLL through direct dialogue with the North, using the momentum made in the Six-Party Talks.

The above recommendations may not be easy to put into practice; however, progress made in these efforts will contribute to the South's successful hosting of the G20 Summit in November 2010. The South needs to consider diverse alternatives in a spirit of open-mindedness, while bearing in mind that there are many variables in its relationship with the North despite the obvious difficulties.

* JPI PeaceNet No.18 published on July 27, 2010 in Korean

Changes in the Internal Situation of North Korea and the Need for Crisis Management in the Transitional Period

CHIN Haeng-Nam
Jeju Peace Institute

It is not easy to know what is happening in North Korea, as it is a closed society and its internal situation can change at any moment. Still, several factors concerning its internal situation are not so hard to guess as stated in the following:

▌ Several Factors Concerning North Korea's Internal Situation

First of all, the country should establish a new system led by Kim Jong-il's heir-apparent very rapidly due to the dictator's poor health. The country held a Supreme People's Council meeting twice this year. Holding the council meetings more than once a year is unprecedented. It plans to hold the Korean Workers Party (KWP) Delegates' Conference in September after an interval of 44 years. The series of recent steps taken by North Korea appear to be aimed at blocking the possibility of instability of the regime in the course of the power transfer and filling loopholes.

Second, the country's internal situation has become instable due to the prevalent bitter sentiment among the people following the failure of the recent currency reform. In the past, the regime would not have minded the grassroots sentiment. However, it should now use "carrots" to have grassroots rally to the support of the new leader. However, it will not be easy for North Korea to do it due to the worsening economic difficulty. Early this year, Kim Jong-il admitted that he had failed to fulfill his deceased father's wish "for having the people eat white rice and meat soup until their stomach is full."

Third, the North Korean regime tends to depend more on hard power apparently to stabilize its internal situation. It is said that high-ranking officials in North Korea were shot to death in public. Pak Nam-gi, a high-ranking official in the Korean Workers' Party in charge of financial affairs, is also said to have been shot on a charge of failure in the currency reforms. It shows the decrease in the number of soft power resources in the country and the weakening of the solidarity within the system.

Fourth, operation of the ruling system in North Korea is being interrupted due to the rapid distribution of information in the markets, a change in the dominant social value appearing in the form of political indifference and materialistic pursuit, and confusion between the private and public sectors. They appear to affect the internal situation considerably, thus weakening the durability of the regime.

There are also other factors that may affect the internal situation of North Korea, including the power struggle between the party and the military over the heir apparent and internal and foreign policies. The above-said factors appear to be in synergistic interaction with each other to drive North Korea's regime into a state of transitional crisis.

▌ How the U.S. and China Cope with the Transitional Crisis

The ripple effect caused by the transitional crisis in North Korea on the entire Korean Peninsula and Northeast Asia is by no means small. Some experts think that the Cheonan Incident in March 2010 was a result of the outward projection of such a serious internal situation of North Korea. They say that the incident of attacking a southern naval ship was more than retaliation of its loss in a previous naval skirmish. The attack on the Cheonan might have been one of its choices designed to rally internal solidarity by giving vent to pent up discontent and unease about the internal situation and justify the transfer of power from Kim Jong-il to one of his sons.

North Korea is still holding on to the slogan of construction of a militarily strong country, but time is not on its side. South Korea should not overlook the fact that North Korea's leadership may perpetrate something more serious due to the obsession that it should show something to its people by a deadline that it promised. The South Koreans are given a heavy task concerning how to manage North Korea's regime going through the transitional crisis.

China's attitude of putting the stability of the Korean Peninsula ahead of North Korea's nuclear weapons appears to be its own management strategy concerning the transitional period in North Korea. Needless to say, China thinks that the stability of the Korean Peninsula is essential for its continued economic development and thus it places priority on it in consideration of its national interest. China insists on a prompt resumption of the Six-Party Talks for a stable management of the situation on the Korean Peninsula. Simultaneously, China appears to be intent on playing a leading role in affairs concerning Northeast Asia and keeping in check the U.S. presence in the region that has grown higher following the Cheonan Incident.

The hypersensitive response made by China to the combined U.S.-South Korea naval exercises carried out after the Cheonan incident shows that the Korean Peninsula issue can turn into a game played by neighboring powers. That is to say, the Cheonan incident provided the material for a tug of war for the influence on Northeast Asia between the U.S. and China, although it is basically an issue to be settled between the two Koreas.

Recently, the U.S. took a "not too harsh, not too gentle" strategy, adopting a non-compulsive administrative order, against North Korea unlike the intensive sanction against Iran under the domestic law. It is interpreted as a consideration not to block the exit for North Korea that may finally return to the sincere-hearted dialogue with the international community, although such a measure takes the vicious cycle of financial sanctions against North Korea and its nuclear test into account.

▌Considerations to be Made for North Korea-related Policy Following the Cheonan Incident

The sensitiveness felt by South Koreans to North Korea's nuclear program is clearly different from that felt by the Chinese. The logic of coping with the transitional crisis in North Korea and methods adopted by the two countries cannot help but be basically different from each other. Granted, South Korea cannot let the transitional crisis issue, which can be compared to a "time bomb," go unattended under the reality of the relations between the two Koreas. Before long, time will come for the South Korean government to seriously consider an exit strategy concerning the Cheonan incident, including the resumption of the dialogue with North Korea.

Nonetheless, the possibility of the early resumption of a dialogue between the authorities of the two Koreas looks slim due to the enormous shock and outrage felt by South Koreans. Thus, the South Korean government needs to consider supplying rice to North Koreans through a third party, like the WFP, in connection with their dire needs. It is not desirable to try to apply a strictly reciprocal measure, either on humanitarian grounds or in connection with the need to win the heart of North Korean residents. It will also be worth trying to restore exchanges and collaboration between the two Koreas in the private sector. The two Koreas are destined not to be separated from each other completely, no matter what may come. The South Korean government should set up a closely-knit strategy in preparation for a two-track proposal of "sanctions and dialogue" made by the U.S.

* JPI PeaceNet No.20 published on August 11, 2010 in Korean

Development of the ROK-Russia Relations Following the Cheonan Incident and Crucial Issues

PARK Chong-Soo
St. Petersburg State University

The Cheonan incident, which occurred on March 26, 2010, made the worldwide attention focus on the Korean Peninsula. That is because of the geopolitical characteristics of the peninsula where the interests of neighboring countries are acutely in conflict with each other. The South Korean (SK) Government concentrated on defining the cause of the incident objectively by launching an international joint investigation team including the U.S., the U.K., Australia, Sweden and Indonesia, but not including Russia and China. In his statement on May 24, SK President Lee Myung-bak said that the incident was caused by a North Korea's torpedo attack. He called Russian President Dmitry Medvedev, explaining the whole picture of the incident and asking for Russia's dispatch of an investigation team. In addition, the SK Government made diplomatic efforts to secure the international community's support for the country's position in the Cheonan incident. A Russian delegation made its own investigation for a week starting on June 1 and returned home. The SK Government expected that the Russian government would make a positive response concerning its referral of a proposal for sanctions against North Korea to the UN Security Council (UNSC). The UNSC adopted its President's statement accusing the attack of the Cheonan, but failed to pinpoint North Korea as the aggressor due to the opposition of Russia and China. It is said that President Lee Myung-bak expressed a great disappointment at such an attitude from Russia. He had made efforts to establish business relations with Russia even before the two countries normalized their diplomatic relations in 1990. He has also strived to establish friendly relations with Russia since he was sworn in as Korean President and held Summits with the Russian President on several occasions. It is understandable that he felt betrayed by such an attitude from Russia. However, inter-country relations are often accompanied by conflicts and reconciliations. One needs to analyze the cause of conflicts in a cool-headed, objective and realistic way.

Let's think about the following factors: First of all, South Koreans might have overlooked the basic characteristics of Russians in their relations with Russia over the past 20 years. Russians are characterized by cautiousness and leisureliness. During the Soviet period, they did not mind standing in a long line to buy a loaf of bread in a sub-zero temperature. Perhaps, such a mindset was developed due to the country's specific geopolitical position and history of hardship. In contrast, Koreans are short-tempered and full of energy. The SK Government set up a roadmap on the referral of sanctions against North Korea to the UNSC and waited to hear news of the result of the Russian delegation's investigation on the Cheonan. In short, South Korea expected too much.

Second, South Koreans should have paid more attention to procedural factors and diplomatic skills in the efforts to secure the cooperation of other countries on the Cheonan incident. If their government decided to exclude Russians and Chinese in the international investigation team, it should have persuaded them concerning the inevitability of the choice through diplomatic efforts. SK President Lee Myung-bak took the trouble of calling the Russian President to explain the background of the launch of the team. SK mass media reported, based on the announcement made by the Cheongwadae, that President Medvedev of Russia called SK President Lee Myung-bak, telling him that Russia was ready to cooperate closely with the SK Government on the Cheonan incident. However, on May 25, the Kremlin homepage carried a statement "разговор состоялся по инициативе южнокорейской стороны" ("The phone call was made by SK.") Is this a matter that can be overlooked as insignificant?

In connection with Russia's positive response to the SK Government's request for the dispatch of an investigation team, Russia got the advantage of being invited to involve itself in a security-related pending issue concerning the Korean Peninsula, including the Cheonan incident, although belatedly. It appears that the South Koreans' impatience in urging Russia to disclose the result of its investigation on the Cheonan incident resulted in an undesirable situation due to the indiscreet way of a diplomatic approach. Such an attitude drove the matter astray from the need to confirm North Korea as the culprit and gave an excuse to Russia, which did not want to antagonize North Korea.

Third, the issue of terrorism is closely associated with Russia's sense of pride, as a country that has been harassed by Chechen rebels' terrorism following the collapse of the Soviet Union. Only a few months ago, a large-scale terror attack was made in a subway station in downtown Moscow. In his Presidential inaugural speech in 2000, Vladimir Putin asked the international community to form a joint front against terrorism, predicting that the 21st Century would see the humankind beleaguered by terrorism. Russia's FSB (Federal Security Service), which replaced the KGB of the Soviet period, has held a large-scale international anti-terrorism conference every year since 2002, inviting intelligence agencies from the world over. The country has accumulated considerable knowhow in return for the expense it paid. The accumulated knowhow means a strong sense of pride. The country's characteristically cautious attitude plus the heavy burden as a country that has accumulated a considerable knowhow in terrorism would have made it difficult for the country to join in the international community's finger pointing at North Korea as the culprit of the Cheonan incident.

The Cheonan incident can be said to be an example that shows the current status of the bilateral diplomatic relations between SK and Russia. SK's heavy dependence on the alliance with the U.S. has left problems in its relations with other friendly countries. Tens of years have passed since the publication of Daniel Bell's book "The End of Ideology." Socialist countries collapsed one after another and the cold war period was over. And SK resumed diplomatic relations with Russia in 1990 and with China in 1992. However, they still appear to live with the cold war mindset. Perhaps, those on the Korean Peninsula are engaged in acts that cause the advent of a neo cold war period. There is no way to survive with analog technology in the era of digital technology. SK may have to see the repetition of incidents similar to the Cheonan, if it loses grip on the power balance as a country surrounded by powers. They should never forget the lesson left by the history of the end of Imperial Korea (1897-1910), which became the arena of competition of powers.

Then, what is a desirable way for South Korea to mend fences with Russia in the wake of the Cheonan incident? Fundamental efforts, including the following, should be made:

First, SK should strive to secure talented people well-versed in relations with Russia. The country does not have a sufficient number of experts on Russia although 20 years have passed since the resumption of diplomatic relations with it. As for China, SK required many experts on China during the cold war period due to the existence of Taiwan and there were many Korean-Chinese who spoke Korean. In contrast, the country did not have many experts on Russia. Even after the reestablishment of diplomatic relations with it, the people of the country made little of Russia, as it lost the status as a superpower, following the collapse of the Soviet Union. It led to the failure to train experts on Russia. To make the matter worse, there were only a small number of ethnic Koreans in Russia who spoke Korean. Diplomacy should not be monopolized by a small number of high-ranking officials, including the President. With the infrastructure remaining weak, the will of the leader cannot be delivered properly. It is doubtful how many experts on Russia there are among high-ranking SK officials in charge of diplomacy and security. It is high time that the country should pay more attention to this problem. If the solution of the problem is left to the market, the country may end up jeopardizing its future.

Second, South Koreans should stop viewing Russia only from their own perspective. They should not repeat the past folly like King Gojong taking refuge at the Russian Legation in Seoul for a year, feeling threatened by the Japanese between February 1896 and February 1897. The country's fate, including the division into South Korea and North Korea, has often been swayed by outside powers, due to the geopolitical factors influencing the peninsula. It would be foolish of South Koreans not to be able to maintain good relations with Russia due to the deep-rooted communist-phobia. If the SK Government expected Russia to play an auxiliary role for it concerning the referral of the Cheonan incident to the UNSC, it was an act of naïveté. Russia is a permanent member of the UNSC that is recovering its status as a world power, overcoming the transitional confusion it had gone through toward the end of the last century. The Russian authorities think that North Korea's leadership will not be intimidated by the international community's sanctions concerning the Cheonan incident and that such sanctions do not help settle the incident.

Third, it is time that SK should set up an exit strategy in the wake of the Cheonan incident. The incident may remain unsettled forever under international law and the country should not let such an incident pose a stumbling block in its relations with Russia. The country should learn a lesson from the Gulf of Tonkin Incident in August 1964. The U.S. insisted that its naval ship was attacked by North Vietnamese torpedo boats and that gave it an excuse to start open warfare against North Vietnam. The war of attrition, which lasted for years, was finally ended with a defeat for the U.S. It is also necessary to pay attention to the Russian Navy's submarine Kursk that sank in the Barents Sea after an explosion in August 2000. The Putin regime of Russia, which was just inaugurated, was faced with a great political crisis, but Putin succeeded in turning the misfortune into a blessing.

It is not wise to continue arguing endlessly just because the result of the Russians' investigation is not something that the SK Government expected. The ceremony held last April in the Bolshoi Theater to commemorate the 20th anniversary of the resumption of the diplomatic relations between the two countries was devoid of merry-making atmosphere under the specter of the Cheonan incident. Various events held for a similar purpose in the ensuing 7-month period failed to attract enthusiasm of the people of the two countries. The Korea-Russia Dialogue Forum and the closing ceremony of the events are slated for early November right before the G20 Summit. The forum, which will be attended by the leaders of the two countries, can serve as a momentum for the development of the bilateral relations and an opportunity for the restoration of mutual trust. SK should fully utilize it as an opportunity to put an end to the awkward situation in its relations with Russia caused by the Cheonan incident.

---

* JPI PeaceNet No.21 published on August 25, 2010 in Korean

Provision of Humanitarian Support to North Korea

KWON Tae-jin
Korea Rural Economic Institute

This year, the weather on the Korean Peninsula has been quite bizarre. Strong winds accompanying Typhoon Kompasu, which took an unusual course, hit Seoul and its vicinity, dealing a severe blow to people who have rarely been victims of a typhoon in the past. On the eve of Chuseok (Chuseok is one of the typical traditional holidays in Korea), a record downpour (100mm of precipitation per hour in some areas) also hit Seoul and its vicinity, resulting in many flood victims. North Korea was also hit by heavy rainfall on roughly five occasions between mid-July and early September, resulting in numerous flood victims and considerable loss of property. It is reported that Sineuiju (Shinuiju is a city located in the lower reaches of the Amnokgang River in Pyeonganbuk-do, North

Korea) suffered a particularly severe loss. The North's government asked the South for rice, cement and excavators, in addition to accepting the South's proposal of relief aid worth 10 billion Korean Won (USD 9 million) for flood victims. It also proposed a session of reunion between separated family members dispersed throughout the two Koreas.

▌Cause of North Korea's Chronic Food Shortage

The North's request for food made to the National Red Cross of the South and proposal for another session of reunions between dispersed families is somewhat unusual given what it has done in the past. It has rarely asked specifically for rice. The two Koreas have exchanged no dialogue for a long time amid an atmosphere of hostility. The flood may turn out to be a factor that will help them put an end to such an awkward situation.

The North's food shortage is the result of human failures. Severe natural disasters have also been a result of policy failure. However, no one can openly blame the country's leader for policy failure under the prevailing authoritarian system. Its ruling class has laid the blame for the food shortage on natural disaster in an attempt to allay people's discontent.

It was already expected that the North would suffer a food shortage by a margin of more than one million tons of grains following the failed harvest in 2009. In 2004, the North announced that it would not accept food relief from the international community any longer. Its food shortage was expected from that time on, as it was a well-known fact that the country did not have the ability to resolve the food shortage problem on its own. The country has also perpetrated certain regrettable acts—including nuclear tests and the launch of missiles—that have inflamed the international community's disapproval.

▌Rules for Humanitarian Support

South Korea became a member of the OECD's Development Assistance Committee (DAC) in 2009, thus making the transition from a recipient to a donor country. There was a controversy over how to provide aid to needy countries due to the possibility that international aid might help dictators remain in power longer rather than actually helping the people most in need. Countries in Asia and Africa are often pointed out as examples of this particular problem. In December, 1991, the UN General Assembly established specific principles for the provision of humanitarian support to avoid such a problem. The following three principles are particularly important concerning food aid.

First, a would-be recipient country should ask for aid first. A country suffering a disaster should be primarily responsible for humanitarian issues concerning its people and should ask for other countries' aid if necessary. This procedure is required to ensure its sovereignty.

Second, the beneficiaries of humanitarian aid should be defined clearly. In many cases, the beneficiaries are limited to those in a specific area or class of the country suffering a disaster. This procedure will help maximize the effect of humanitarian aid.

Third, it should be checked whether the aid has been provided to the specified beneficiaries. Through such a process of monitoring, the aid can be provided efficiently in addition to enhancing the transparency of aid distribution.

The foregoing principles should apply to rehabilitation aid or development aid as well as to food relief aid as for flood victims. Development aid requires more stringent principles and complicated procedures than relief aid. Even in the case of the South's provision of aid for flood victims in the North, consultation on how to keep these principles should come first concerning rice and other relief items provided by the South. It seems ludicrously inappropriate to offer a session of reunion between members of dispersed families in return for relief aid.

What made the North propose such an initiative at this juncture? When there is a need to provide food aid to the North, the Government should adhere to these principles so that it may reach a consensus among the people and gain the trust of the international community.

I Need to Link Relief Aid with Development Aid

Relief aid is a measure taken to improve an urgent situation on humanitarian grounds. The unfavorable weather conditions on the Korean Peninsula this summer are a sign of an even more difficult food situation for Northerners next year. The North will require more aid from the international community next year and possibly in the years ahead.

To bring about a fundamental improvement of the food shortage problem in the North, the international community's development aid should be promoted while the North should make efforts of its own. Efforts should also be made to improve the humanitarian situation in the North. The country should be made to show any efforts made in that direction to the international community as a precondition for development aid. The North should be made to realize that it can only obtain international community's development aid if it acts as a responsible member of the international community.

The specific relations between the two Koreas need to be considered with regard to the provision of aid to the North, but that should not be stressed excessively. If the South acts in a way that is unacceptable in light of international norms in its provision of aid to the North, the international community will regard it as an immature act. Any acts that violate the principles and norms set by the international community will only serve as inhibitors of the peace and prosperity that humankind aims for. Some people say that even humanitarian aid should take political factors into account, but the country will be regarded as a mature member of the international community when it strives to reduce the connectivity between humanitarian considerations and the political situation. As the host country of the G20 Summit this coming November, the country should carry out the relevant acts as a responsible member of the international community.

---

* JPI PeaceNet No.25 published on September 27, 2010 in Korean

North Korea's Diplomatic Policy toward the US: Its Recent Moves

CHA Du-hyeon
Korea Foundation

On August 25, 2010, former U.S. President Jimmy Carter paid a visit to Pyongyang and succeeded in obtaining the release of an American citizen, Aijalon Gomes, who entered the country on a religious mission without the prior approval of the North Korean authorities, from a 7-month-long period of custody in North Korea. Thus, the two countries actually made a successful attempt at communication, although Jimmy Carter confined the purpose of his visit to its humanitarian purpose i.e. the release of an American from custody, and was unable to meet North Korean leader Kim Jong-il, as former President Bill Clinton did during his visit to the country in 2009.

▌North Korea's "Hostage Diplomacy": an Intended Tactic or Sheer Chance?

What is interesting is the fact that the situation surrounding Jimmy Carter's visit to the North was quite similar to Bill Clinton's in 2009. All official dialogue channels between the two countries remained closed and it was difficult to find an exit from the stalemate caused by the North's hostile foreign policy, including the test launch of long-range missiles and the second nuclear test (2009), as well as the Cheonan Incident (2010). However, the fact remains that a former U.S. leader paid a visit to the capital of the North, when the two countries were slowly accelerating their invisible diplomatic overtures toward the resumption of dialogue. The U.S. still holds to the position that it can hardly take a step to resume dialogue with the North unless the North adopts a sincere attitude toward the Cheonan Incident, but it is clear that all the countries involved, including the North, are considering an exit strategy following the Cheonan Incident.

Bill Clinton's visit to the North in 2009 served as a catalyst for thawing the strained bilateral relations in the second half of that year, although it did not develop into full-blown bilateral dialogue. In the ensuing period, the North allowed Hyundai Asan Chairman Hyun Jeong-eun to visit the country and dispatched its delegation to pay condolences at the funeral of the late President Kim Dae-jung. The two Koreas agreed to a session of reunion among the dispersed families during Chuseok holidays. The guess that there is something more than a personal visit to Jimmy Carter's trip to the North is based on lessons learned from the past. To say the least, the North utilized the situation caused by an American who entered the country without prior approval to show that it held a flexible position toward the possibility of resuming dialogue and to deliver a message of some kind or other to the U.S. The pieces of the puzzle were assembled so intricately that some observers were led to think that the North might have adopted the hostage diplomacy as a crucial tool of its policy toward the U.S.

It would be out of place to conclude that the North deliberately took an American hostage for use in its diplomacy toward the U.S. One may fall into a cyclical theory error, confusing causal relations with correlations, if one becomes engrossed in such a view. When two American reporters, Yuna Lee and Laura Ling, were arrested by the North Korean military on a charge of crossing the national border in 2009, the North was suspected of acting thus intentionally. In contrast, the case of Gomes was apparently a genuine instance of illegal entry into the country. It is also hard to explain why the North did not use Robert Park, who was also arrested by the North for illegal entry ahead of Gomes and released after two months, if the North intended to use an American civilian as a diplomatic hostage. Nonetheless, it is a cogent explanation to say that the North is making painstaking efforts to resume dialogue with the U.S. for an earlier establishment of direct bilateral relations and tried to use the "hostages" to break out of the stalemate. The North's recent promotion of Kang Seok-ju, Kim Gye-gwan, and Lee Yong-ho, who are referred to as the "Gang of Three" in its diplomacy toward the U.S., can also be interpreted as a step taken in its future approach toward the U.S. It should be borne in mind that a "hostage" situation involving the North provides an opportunity for the U.S. to contact the North without having to consider the position of South Korea as it involves a humanitarian issue.

❙ Relations between the U.S. and North Korea: Changes in the Way Each Views the Other and Factors of Conflicts

An observer of the strategies which the North adopts toward the U.S. needs to monitor any changes in the ways the U.S. and the North view each other, along with any factors of conflict. To the North, the U.S. was one of the overriding stumbling blocks to its "revolution on the Korean Peninsula" during the Cold War. The U.S. was a target that the North had to avoid and defeat. However, throughout the 1990s and the ensuing period, the U.S. began to emerge gradually as a crucial factor for its survival to the eyes of the North's leaders. The North could not help but acknowledge the supremacy of the U.S., which became the only superpower in the world, following the collapse of the Soviet Union and the liberalization of the countries of Eastern Europe. The North also recognized that the formation of normal relations with the international economic order led by the U.S. was the key to extricating itself from dire economic difficulty. Thus, the North adopted a policy of seeking positive dialogues with the U.S. around the time of its leader Kim Il-sung's death in 1994, while employing the brinkmanship tactic, reinforcing its leverage against the U.S. in an effort to cope with the U.S.-led world order. The North used its nuclear weapons and ballistic missiles as a tool of negotiation in its relations with the U.S. under an initiative focused on blocking the U.S. policy aimed at regime change in the North and the establishment of direction relations with the North to maximize its gains.

Such a change in the North's attitude toward the U.S., coupled with a change in the U.S. view of the North, resulted in the formation of factors of both conflict and the need for collaboration between the two countries. During the Cold War, the North was no more than a proxy of the Soviet Union and China in this part of the world. It appears that in the early post-Cold War period the U.S. viewed the North as a regime that would follow the fate of Eastern Europe or the Soviet Union (i.e., as one that would experience collapse or regime change), although it was in possession of WMDs, including nuclear weapons, as a peripheral rogue state. However, following 9/11 in 2001, the U.S. started to view the North as an opponent to be reckoned with realistically rather than as a faraway threat. That is, the North became an opponent that the U.S. would have to cope with either through regime change or mutual collaboration in a period in which a regime or a group of people equipped with WMDs or strong animosity toward the U.S. can threaten the security of the U.S. more than a powerful country can.

▌The U.S. Exit Strategy Following the Cheonan Incident

One thing that South Korea should keep in mind is that it is difficult to expect the U.S. to take a course of action concerning the North in a way that would be completely satisfactory to it to the end despite the series of measures taken showing the solid mutual collaboration between the countries following the Cheonan Incident. In the period immediately following the incident, the U.S. took the position that "there are no grounds to suspect the North's involvement," but gradually changed its view, pointing to diverse possibilities. In mid-April and thereafter, the U.S. supported the South's position positively, emphasizing the importance of the mutual collaboration between the two countries. Such an approach on the part of the U.S. appears to stem from the need for collaboration with the South and for realistic gains from its policy toward the North simultaneously. Suspicion of the North's involvement in the Cheonan Incident was a useful card that the U.S. could play to persuade the North to return to the Six-Party Talks, at a time when the existing preconditions (such as the Peace Treaty for the Korean Peninsula or mitigation of sanctions against the North) had been withdrawn, and against China, a traditional guardian of the North. The U.S. might have thought that with such a card it could force the North to yield on the adoption of the denuclearization verification protocol, which was a major cause of the collapse of the Six-Party Talks in December 2008. The U.S. appears to have stepped up its pressure on the North, including the imposition of additional sanctions, since the Cheonan Incident, but they are really no more than a response to the North's WMDs and hardly constitute punitive measures for its attack on the South Korean naval ship Cheonan.

The U.S. currently has a mountain of controversial domestic issues to overcome, such as reform of its medical insurance and financial systems, to which it should pay full attention. As such, the country does not have sufficient capacity to concentrate on foreign policy. Moreover, Iran's nuclear program and the unstable situation in the Middle East are more serious issues than the issue concerning the Korean Peninsula. Under such circumstances, the U.S. may find it more advantageous to its national interest to maintain a certain level of dialogue with the North, while trying to manage the situation in such a way that the North cannot perpetrate more extreme actions (such as a third nuclear test), rather than sticking to a hard-line policy against the North.

Such a possibility is indicated by the diplomatic moves recently taken by the North and its neighboring countries. Accordingly, South Korea needs to start contemplating how to conclude the situation following the Cheonan Incident, now that discussion is in full flow about the resumption of the Six-Party Talks.

---

* JPI PeaceNet No.26 published on October 1, 2010 in Korean

It is Time to Consider an Exit Strategy concerning the Cheonan Incident

KIM Jin-Ho
Jeju National University

It is not an exaggeration to say that the news concerning the country has been dominated by the Cheonan Incident over the past six months. Nonetheless, the situation surrounding the Korean Peninsula has continued changing, including the dynamics caused by North Korean leader Kim Jong-il's visits to China in May and August this year. The speed of the changes is enough to make an observer's head swim.

Amid such circumstances, the country's government announced a series of measures concerning the future of the Korean Peninsula, including a proposal for the imposition of a "unification tax." Recently, a Presidential aide said, "The Government is seeking a gradual approach toward peaceful unification based on the consent of the two Koreas. It is wrong to say that liberals want the unification of the country, while conservatives hope that the country will remain divided. Unification is the ultimate wish of Koreans, liberals and conservatives alike. In this sense, the President's speech commemorating the country's liberation from colonial rule on August 15 served as an occasion to encourage people to take part in discussions about unification." (The Tongil Shinmun newspaper dated September 6, 2010). It happened that Sinuiju, North Korea, suffered from heavy flooding, whereupon many people in the South said that the South should provide humanitarian support to the flood victims in the North, voicing their view that the South should collaborate with the North where possible, separating it from the country's political and military stance.

Recently, the North proposed a session of reunions of members of dispersed families, when the South was considering the provision of humanitarian support to it. The proposal appears to be a tactic designed to soften the South's hard-line stance following the Cheonan Incident. The North appears to be trying to find a means to restore collaborative relations with the South and to improve its relations with the U.S. The North has fully mobilized its diplomatic capabilities in a bid to alleviate the international community's sanctions following the UN Security Council's

Presidential Statement on the Cheonan Incident. (The Tongil Shinmun newspaper dated September 20, 2010).

The Cheonan Incident revealed that the current national security status of the country leaves much to be desired. The relevant ministries of the South Korean Government showed that they were not quite ready to cope with national security threats. The military disclosed that its chain of command was at a level far from satisfactory. People saw that there were many limitations to what the Government could do in its relations with other countries. All these left people with a deep sense of distrust toward the Government. Nevertheless, the efforts made by the Government on the diplomatic front following the Cheonan Incident appear to have garnered substantial results. To say the least, the UN Security Council's Presidential Statement on the Cheonan Incident is significant in that it has served to remind the member countries of the situation on the Korean Peninsula. Meantime, the Government should adopt an approach toward the North's apology for its attack on the Cheonan in a different way to that which what it has tried so far in connection with the need to carry out a more mature diplomacy as a country hosting the G20 Summit in November 2010, keeping the following in mind:

First of all, the current Lee Myung-bak Administration now has only two years and a few months to go. It is time for the administration to check its performance results and keep them in perspective. It should be able to present a noticeable improvement in the country's preparedness against a contingency like the Cheonan Incident to the public some time within this year. Only then can the ruling party be in a favorable position in the National Assembly and Presidential elections in 2012. If the administration fails to do that, the country will undergo another series of conflicts. Failure to establish a more mature political culture will damage the overall political and diplomatic capability of the country.

Second, As for the position adopted by both South Korea and the U.S. that the North's apology concerning the Cheonan Incident should precede the resumption of the Six-Party Talks, the possible approach on the minds of the two countries is as follows: improvement of the relations between the two Koreas→ contacts between the U.S. and the North→preliminary meetings→ resumption of the Six-Party Talks. The situation requires a shift in the role of the South Korean Government and its policy. It is expected that the new Prime Minister and Foreign Minister will start carrying out their respective duties soon. Upon completion of the lineup of the new cabinet, the Government should seek a change in its diplomatic and security policies. Meantime, China and North Korea appeared to display continuing friendly relations at a summit held in a northeastern province of China toward the end of August.

Third, there was a change in the North's officials in charge of diplomacy. Vice Foreign Minister Kang Seok-ju, who led the country's nuclear-related negotiations and diplomacy toward the U.S., was promoted to Vice Prime Minister, according to the North Korean Central News Agency on September 23. It appears that the North considers generational change concerning those in charge of nuclear-related negotiations, while stressing the importance of the diplomacy toward the U.S. Those promoted this time are officials who have accumulated experience concerning nuclear-related negotiations and diplomacy toward the U.S. in the North's Foreign Ministry. Kang Seok-ju is one of the North's representative experts in the said areas. He has served in the same post for 24 years, and succeeded in concluding the U.S.-DPRK Framework Agreement in 1994. There will be a change in the U.S. policy toward the North, depending on the result of the mid-term election slated for November of this year. The South Korean Government should take a considerate and timely step concerning a change in its policy toward the North, with the prevalent circumstances taken into account, lest it should be blamed as the party that inhibited progress in the Six-Party Talks.

Fourth, it is reported that the meeting of the Workers' Party of North Korea, which was originally slated for early September, will be held on September 28. There will certainly be a change in the leadership of the regime. There are things happening in that country that outsiders cannot understand. Concerning the meeting to be held in Pyongyang, the British mass media said on September 22 that the occasion will be a watershed for the world's most clandestine dictatorship. (The Yonhap News dated September 22, 2010)

Fifth, the G20 Summit is a very important international event that will enhance the prestige of South Korea, which has set an example with its economic growth even amid the worldwide crisis, and apply direct and indirect diplomatic pressure on the North. According to The Yonhap News, a person who paid a visit to Pyongyang to attend the third North Korean Labor Party Delegate Meeting told the North Korean People's Liberation Front, which is an organization composed of North Korean ex-servicemen defectors, that the North's Defense Commission had held a secret meeting to discuss ways to disturb the G20 Summit in Seoul. It is said that when the representatives of the countries involved met to discuss ways to operate the world economic order in a virtuous cycle following the financial crisis in 2008, the North blamed it as a meeting designed to isolate and crush it to death. The report said that, concerning the G20 Summit, the North may consider taking steps to foster an uneasy security-related environment and providing support to demonstrations against the summit held by pro-North groups of people in the South. The necessary steps will be taken by the South Korean Government, but it will also be necessary to persuade the North not to commit such a folly.

Sixth, it is necessary to adopt a positive engagement policy concerning the North, including preventive measures designed for management of the situation related to it. Needless to say, such a measure is in the national interest of the South. The current Lee Myung-bak Administration needs to adopt a new paradigm in its relations with the North. The South needs to reconsider ways to manage issues related to the North and take diplomatic initiatives based on the alliance with the U.S. and the strategic partnership with China. Technically, the two Koreas are in a state of war, but there is no denying the need to ease tension and foster a peaceful environment through dialogue. The South Korean Government should employ wisdom to bring about a change in the situation when the conditions are favorable. We should not forget the tragedy of the Cheonan Incident. Nor should we commit the folly of sticking to it blindly.

---

* JPI PeaceNet No.27 published on October 5, 2010 in Korean

Russian Perspective
on Inter-Korean Relations

Sergey O. KURBANOV
University of St.-Petersburg

Leo Tolstoy once said, "Russians are a peaceful nation; they don't like war." Agree or disagree with this statement, it is interesting that in Russian "world" and "peace" sound the same—"Mir." So for Russians the ideal state of the world is peace.

In 1945, Korea was temporarily divided into two parts to support peace and prosperity. Russia and the United States were allies and friends. In 1945, nobody could imagine that in the near future that they would suddenly become enemies and divide the world into two struggling parts. Korea became part of this division process that began in 1947 and that initiated the Cold War. Korea became the Asian center of this division and became the main struggle of two diametric state systems (socialism and capitalism). The Korean War that followed was one of the most severe wars of the second half of the 20th century.

Russians wish for peace. During the final period of the Soviet Union and right after its collapse, the Russian government did everything to establish diplomatic relations with "former enemies" like the Republic of Korea. Russians supported the destruction of the Berlin Wall and hoped that the 'Korean Wall' built through the middle of the Korean Peninsula will also soon disappear. Russians and all other nations in Eastern Europe recognized the Republic of Korea.

At the same time, neither the United States of America nor Japan recognized North Korea. While the situation became more stable in Europe after the destruction of the Berlin Wall, the non-recognition of North Korea by the United Stated and Japan strengthened the Korean Wall and assisted the continuing discord of the Korean Peninsula.

North Koreans say that it is possible and that it is necessary to solve Korean problems through the efforts of two Koreas only as "one nation." However, it was outside powers that divided Korea and not themselves, in the future the reunification of Korea will depend on outside powers.

Imagine that the United States of America, Japan, Russia, and China suddenly disappeared. As well the space becomes nothing but desert between Korea and Mongolia, Korea and Vietnam, Korea and India, and Korea and Mexico. I think that in this case it would be possible to solve the Korean question through Koreans themselves; however, Korea is not the only nation on Earth. Korea is involved in complicated international relations and has become an important player in world politics. Korea is not able to act in the world arena without understanding this complicated net of international relations and no inter-Korean relations are possible without improving the whole system of international relations with both Koreas.

Russia, China, and Vietnam have already taken steps toward peace on the Korean peninsula. Russia, China, and Vietnam have friendly relations with both the Republic of Korea and with the Democratic People's Republic of Korea. It is time for other remaining countries to recognize North Korea; the Korean Peninsula will establish an international environment that will promote stable inter-Korean relations after the United States of America, Japan, and their allies recognize North Korea with no preliminary conditions.

Russia and Eastern Europe have recognized the Republic of Korea with no preliminary conditions (such as a change from dictatorship to democracy). Others must act in a similar way to recognize North Korea with no preliminary conditions.

How can we neglect the "violation of human rights" and other "big" problems in North Korea? However, what are human rights? Why do North Koreans have no rights to contact Americans? No rights to use iPhones? No rights to listen to the world pop music (North Koreans had a plan to invite Eric Clapton to Pyongyang but this plan was not realized)? These are also a part of the complicated system of "human rights."

I was in Pyongyang in December of 2000, just one month after the United States Secretary of State Madeleine Albright visited Pyongyang. I remember the enthusiastic comments of North Koreans about her visit. When I traveled the winter streets of Pyongyang, schoolchildren passed by and they greeted me in English, thinking that I was an American and were very friendly to me. I felt that despite the official vilification of the United States by the North Korean mass media the North Korean public did not feel any hostility towards to the United States. On the opposite, they dream about establishing peace and firm diplomatic relations with this country and this is only to stabilizing the situation on the Korean Peninsula. Only after establishing such relations, can regular and stable inter-Korean relations become real.

I will prove my statement through one historical example of inter-Korean relations. Everybody remembers the historical visit of former Korean president Kim Dae-jung to Pyongyang in the summer of 2000. Many analysts explained this political achievement through the personal qualities of Kim Dae-jung or by the "financial support" given to North Korea (frequently seen as a "bribe" to the North Korean regime) or by numerous other reasons. At the same time, many analysts forgot about the North Korean policy of US president Bill Clinton at the end of the 1990s and beginning of 2000s. Later this policy was evaluated as "too soft." However, it was the end of 2000 when Pyongyang was full of rumors about an "imminent" visit to Pyongyang by President Bill Clinton and the establishment of diplomatic relations with the United States.

In 2001, some of the problems in the relations of North Korea with the United States and some friction in inter-Korean relations began to appear. When President Kim Dae-jung visited the United States in March of 2001 to meet newly elected US president George Bush, the Korean mass media was informed for the first time about the "gap" in perceptions between Kim Dae-jung and George Bush about the character of the North Korean regime. Since then one can trace the complications of North Korea—US relations and the moderate cooling of relations between the two Koreas.

There are other reasons for the diplomatic recognition of North Korea that surpass the North Korean desire to establish diplomatic relations with the USA. However, the main reason is peace and stability on the Korean Peninsula.

The modern Russian army and weapon systems are not as massive as they were under the Soviet Union. Why and how did it happen? First, the necessity of maintaining a huge military machine disappeared when the "Iron Curtain" that separated the Soviet Union from the democratic world was destroyed. The Russian army then began its transformation; modern Russia is now no longer a threat to anybody in the world.

I think that the North Korean case is the same. I should like to compare modern North Korea with a champagne bottle overloaded by inner pressure and ready to explode. Follow the precautions of opening its cork quietly to let its gas release slowly and you will get a safe bottle with high quality wine. In addition, like Russia that reduced its weapons systems after the end of the "Iron Curtain" the North Korean army will also begin its transformation (together with the songun policy itself) after North Korea opens to the outer world. The magic opener is nothing else but the United States of America.

Only after the international process of stabilization on the Korean

Peninsula begins can the continuous development of inter-Korean relations start to become the reality desired by the ordinary people of both Koreas.

---

* JPI PeaceNet No.29 published on October 19, 2010 in English

【Part 2】

···

Multilateral Cooperation in East Asia

China: Demonstrating that Intentions Follow Capabilities?

Denny ROY
East-West Center

The change is subtle and tentative, but a new phase of U.S.-China relations may be beginning. The change stems from a shift in China's posture, which has otherwise been remarkably consistent since the beginning of the post-Mao era. This shift in turn is an outgrowth of the widely-held expectation that China will take over the U.S. role as the leading power in the region. Beijing seems eager to begin collecting the dividends of this important re-ordering of thee Asia-Pacific power structure.

Deng Xiaoping, the architect of China's post-Mao development strategy and foreign policy, advised his successors in Beijing to avoid taking the lead in foreign affairs and to make peace with

Part 2 Multilateral Cooperation in East Asia *81*

potential adversaries during the long period China would need to build up and modernize its economy to the level of the Western powers. In the 1990s, particularly after the 1999 bombing of the Chinese embassy in Belgrade by NATO aircraft, the Chinese leadership seriously considered taking a more confrontational posture toward the United States. This debate yielded the conclusions that China was not yet strong enough to conduct a cold war with the Americans, that such an approach would jeopardize China's continued rapid economic development by drawing away resources and shutting off opportunities for trade and investment with foreign countries, and that the PRC's best option was to maintain a constructive relationship with the USA unless or until Washington directly challenged a vital Chinese interest (such as intervening in a war over Taiwan independence).

For its part, American policy toward China has also been fairly consistent. U.S. presidential administrations representing both major U.S. political parties have repeatedly said America welcomes a strong, wealthy China on the condition that Beijing's polices are "peaceful" and "responsible." By this they mean Washington will not openly oppose Chinese economic growth as long as China plays within the rules of established (and largely U.S.-sponsored) international norms and institutions. Far from "containing" the PRC as some Chinese often allege, the United States through its trade with China and transfer of technology and expertise has done more than any other country to help China "rise."

Two premises of American economic engagement with China have been that attempting to isolate China economically would backfire by ensuring Chinese hostility, while deepening trade and investment is one of the best means of liberalizing China. Recent American administrations have bought into the theory that democratic countries enter into a political "zone of peace" where war between member countries is obsolete. In case China chooses not to act peacefully or responsibly, the United States maintains the capacity to resist Chinese activities. From the point of view of Washington, therefore, it is justifiable for America to maintain military bases and alliances in the Asia-Pacific region, to take responsibility for ensuring the freedom of the seas, to organize international opposition to regimes that disrespect global norms, to carry out surveillance of Chinese military activities, and to help Taiwan defend itself against the threat of Chinese military action.

The tacit understanding between Beijing and Washington during most of this decade has been that Beijing will not challenge America's status as the pre-eminent Asia-Pacific power or the pillars thereof (including the U.S.-ROK alliance), and Washington will not resist China's growth into a great power as long as Beijing's foreign policies remained peaceful and made progress toward becoming fully "responsible," meaning total convergence with U.S. positions on such issues as non-proliferation and non-support for what Washington considers rogue regimes.

Roughly since the beginning of the global financial crisis, however, a change in the U.S.-China relationship is perceptible. The previous arrangement shows signs of weakening. The current economic crisis began with an asymmetry in the U.S.-China economic relationship in America's favor: despite the massive U.S. trade deficit with China, the Chinese needed this economic partnership more than the Americans did. The reliance of China on the large American market's appetite for Chinese exports gave the Chinese leadership reason to think twice about any possible policies that might damage relations with the USA. The financial crisis, however, has likely hastened the re-balancing of this asymmetry by speeding China's diversification of its overseas markets, increasing America's need for China to finance the U.S. deficit by purchasing Treasury Bonds, reducing the long-term purchasing power of the American consumer, and delegitimizing the Anglo-American approach to financial regulation.

The change did not originate from the U.S. side. The Obama Administration made clear its willingness to continue America's previous posture toward China. It even sweetened the deal by signaling early that it did not intend to let the traditionally divisive issues such as human rights prevent bilateral cooperation on important global matters such as climate change and the economic crisis.

Aadvocates of liberalizing China through engagement and trade have hoped that China would attain a respect for and a commitment to supporting international norms and institutions by the time the Chinese came to believe they were powerful enough that they could choose whether to maintain the current system or overthrow it. If this was a race between China's attainment of great power capabilities and China's becoming socialized to international sensibilities, many observers have warned that the ultimate outcome could be an unfortunate combination of superpower strength, chauvinism and ruthless self-interest.

In departures from Deng's advice, China is becoming more assertive in standing up for its own preferences on questions that do not involve direct threats to vital Chinese interests and in recommending reforms of the international system, even at the risk of harming relations with the United States.

That China would eventually opt for a stronger international leadership role and emerge as a clear rival to American hegemony was not unexpected. Historically, the dominant great power eventually faces a challenge from a rising state with a faster economic growth rate. As the rising challenger's capabilities approach the level of the dominant state's capabilities, the challenger is emboldened to demand greater influence over the rules of international affairs, seeking to reshape these rules (originally written by the old dominant power) to better suit its own interests. Nevertheless, this is happening sooner than some observers anticipated or hoped.

China has recently taken a tougher position in its dispute with Tokyo over an underwater natural gas field in the East China Sea straddling the exclusive economic zone boundaries between China and Japan. Similarly, China has angered Vietnam by announcing plans to develop tourism to the disputed Paracel Islands, which Chinese military forces currently occupy after seizing them from the Vietnamese.

For the United States, the hoped-for convergence of U.S. and Chinese interests seems to be slipping away. China has not warmed to U.S. preferences on human rights or the promotion of democracy worldwide. Beijing still puts forward the principle of "non-intervention" in arguing against American efforts to coordinate international pressure on outlaw governments. While a second North Korean nuclear weapons test forced China to reluctantly go along with a toughened sanctions regime, Beijing quickly compensated with an expanded program of economic cooperation with Pyongyang and generally demonstrated a lack of interest in putting serious pressure on the North Koreans to denuclearize.

In the case of Iran's suspected nuclear weapons program, Beijing obstructed U.S. efforts by insisting on a soft diplomatic approach rather than sanctions. China is increasingly demonstrating a desire to both counter U.S. influence and to take a greater share of global leadership. During the financial crisis, for example, China has criticized the "Washington consensus" and called for an alternative to the U.S. dollar as the primary international currency. The Chinese delegation to the Copenhagen conference on global climate change was unusually bold in its attempts to out-maneuver Washington. And China has recently reacted more strongly than previously to long-standing U.S. policies such as surveillance by U.S. Navy ships off the Chinese coast and American arms sales to Taiwan.

This may signal the end of the period in which the Chinese try to fly under the radar and smooth over differences with over foreign governments while building up their national strength (the spirit of the Chinese aphorism tao guang, yang hui). Deng's ghost is likely displeased, believing it is too early for China to openly challenge the USA and vie for international leadership. The American economy is still nearly three times the size of China's, and the

United States spends as much money on military power as the rest of the world combined. The temptation felt by a rising challenger to speed up the process of hegemonic transition, however, can be overwhelming.

There has never been much doubt that a China that had surpassed the United States in terms of absolute gross national product would be less willing to tolerate perceived affronts to Chinese pride and infringements on Chinese freedom of strategic maneuver. What is surprising here is how quickly this process is unfolding. We can expect that in the coming years a more confident China will demand redress of many additional aspects of international politics in the Asia-Pacific region. U.S. arms sales to Taiwan is one of the first items on a list that also includes the key U.S. alliances in East Asia.

---

* JPI PeaceNet No.1 published on February 6, 2010 in English

Japanese Diplomacy and the Role of Policy Intellectuals: The Significance of the Birth of the DPJ Hatoyama Administration

Katsuhiko NAKAMURA
Asian Forum Japan

Soon, six months will have passed since the birth of the Hatoyama Administration in September 2009. While it can certainly be said that the new government has produced some new directions, it has also led to stagnation in some areas. A symbol of such stagnation is the Hatoyama Administration's handling of the issue of Futenma Air Station relocation and the negative effect that is having on the Japan-US alliance.

January 15 of this year marked the 50th anniversary of the renewal of the Japan-US Security Treaty. However, despite the issue of a joint statement by the foreign ministers and defense ministers of both countries, no joint statement was issued by Japan and US leaders. This is the easiest way to understand the current status of Japan-US relations. An unstable relationship between Japan and the United States will have knock-on effects on the Japan-South Korea relationship and the stability of East Asia. Why has the Hatoyama Administration chosen to bring about this state of affairs?

The answer is that while the Hatoyama Administration talks about creating a "deeper Japan-US alliance," it fails to present specific ideas to actually make the alliance "deeper."

Soon after the start of the year, both the Democratic Party of Japan (DPJ) and the Liberal Democratic Party of Japan (LDP) coincidentally decided to close their party-affiliated think tanks. I am sure I was not the only person who felt surprised that the DPJ, which always talks about "politician-led politics," decided to close its think tank that should be operating as the brain of the party.

In Japan, "Kasumigaseki," where central government ministries are located, has always been described as Japan's largest think tank. If the DPJ is going to talk about politician-led politics, then surely party-affiliated think tanks have a crucial role to play in moderating Kasumigaseki.

In the case of the LDP, we would expect that having lost its grip on power, it would now be more difficult for the party to use Kasumigaseki as the "brain of the party," and a think tank would be even more meaningful as a means of thinking up ideas and strategies to win back power.

In the United States, ideas are not to be taken lightly as they produce results, as stated in Richard M. Weaver's "Ideas Have Consequences" published in 1948. There, policy intellectuals play a major role.

In contrast to public intellectuals who aim to influence the society by appealing to the wider public, policy intellectuals are only involved in actual political debates and propose policies. Since policy intellectuals have a direct and indirect effect on the policy-making process, they must take greater responsibility for their arguments.

By bringing their ideas to fruition, policy intellectuals go beyond the current reality, in other words, they help to open up and create the new reality. Producing output which has high political implications and actually influencing the political decision-making process is the mission, indeed the lifeline, of policy intellectuals.

In other words, policy intellectuals should be aware that ideas that do not go beyond the current situation will simply be treated lightly. Of course, policy intellectuals have a responsibility for working together with politicians to realize their ideas. That responsibility is also required of the politicians who have decided to take on the ideas. And then, a place where policy intellectuals gather together is what we should call a think tank, which is a focus of knowledge or a group for proposing policies.

Up until now, the role of policy intellectuals and think tanks in Japan has mainly been played by the bureaucracy in Kasumigaseki. That was the major characteristic of the Japanese approach. However, as is well known, bureaucrats lack the ability to deal with rapid changes in society. Since they find it difficult to adapt flexibly, the result is the avoidance of responsibility. Last year, following the change of government and the announcement of a move away from bureaucrat-led politics to politician-led politics, we are seeing the role of bureaucrats as policy intellectuals coming to an end.

The problem is that while bureaucrats' roles as policy intellectuals are coming to an end, the politicians who are supposed to be leading the way are failing to foster policy intellectuals and the required ideas.

We hear that just like in the United States, South Korea also has properly functioning think tanks such as the Jeju Peace Institute

(JPI). If Japan is going to claim politician-led politics, then surely we need to foster policy intellectuals who can provide new ideas and develop think tanks that will accumulate those ideas and move to put them in the action.

The birth of the Hatoyama Administration and the change of government in Japan is likely to prove to be an opportunity for a major change in Japan's policy environment.

---

* JPI PeaceNet No.2 published on February 22, 2010 in English

"Greater Tumen Initiative" and Cooperation in Northeast Asia

Nataliya YACHEISTOVA

UNDP/Tumen Secretariat

▌ Greater Tumen Initiative—A Unique Cooperative Mechanism

In terms of intergovernmental cooperation in Northeast Asia (NEA) the Greater Tumen Initiative programme (GTI) may serve as a unique model of intergovernmental cooperation. GTI (originally known as the Tumen River Area Development Programme—TRADP) was created in 1995 on the basis of the intergovernmental agreements among five NEA countries—Democratic People's Republic of Korea, People's Republic of China, Republic of Korea, Mongolia and Russian Federation, with the support of the United Nations Development Programme (UNDP). The main goal of GTI is to promote economic cooperation in Northeast Asia (with a special focus on the Tumen River cross-border area), in order to achieve greater growth and sustainable development for the people and countries in the region.

Since its creation GTI remains a platform for multilateral economic cooperation, contributing to economic growth, peace and stability in the region. For the Tumen Region, which partly consists of remote and landlocked areas of large countries, regional cooperation is an effective way to ensure economic growth and to improve living standards. Regional cooperation is a vital part of the development process and a building block for effective participation in world trade and capital markets. Cross-border cooperation helps to ensure energy security, improve basic infrastructures, develop tourism and adopt international environmental standards in the member countries.

The meetings of the Consultative Commission—the main institutional structure of GTI—provide the unique platform for intergovernmental exchanges among the member countries. The coordination of GTI activities on daily basis is undertaken by the Tumen Secretariat (based in Beijing), which is transforming the decisions, taken by the GTI Consultative Commission, into the practical actions. The Secretariat is guided by the CC Chairperson, and is functioning in close cooperation with the member countries and UNDP. The GTI cooperation is actively supported not only by GTI central governments, but also by regional and local authorities, NGOs and business community throughout the world.

I Promoting Economic Peaceful Cooperation in Northeast Asia

The NEA region has enormous potential for investment and job opportunities with its rich mineral resources, advantageous geographical situation and skilled, educated and competitive labor pool. But this potential could be fully realized only through joined efforts and common will.

The regional trade and investments in NEA were growing very quickly in the recent years, driven by easy access to cheap capital and high international consumer demand. The financial crisis transferred these tendencies into a sharp decline in FDI inflows and exports as a result of collapsed global demand. However, NEA has a huge potential to grow, and according to some estimates, the NEA region will recover from the economic crisis more quickly and with less negative consequences than other regions of the world. Many of NEA economies have high savings, moderate debts and have introduced impressive stimulus packages which will help them to overcome the negative consequences of the crisis.

In order to facilitate the economic recovery, the world leaders have agreed to abstain from protectionism and not to introduce the new trade barriers. Nevertheless, the Northeast Asia region still remains bounded with a lot of restrains; its the only region in the world without internal Free Trade Agreements and it doesn't have any proper institutional platform for joint cooperation (like ASEAN in Southeast Asia). The Northeast Asia countries have not yet harmonized their investment regulations, resulting in a limited number of large-scale trans-border investment projects. Such situation keeps the business community restrained from high investments, keeping business in uncertainty, expecting further improvements and the creation of predictable and homogeneous business conditions in this region. To promote economic growth, trade and investment, a stronger regional cooperation in NEA is needed (which could be a unique opportunity for NEA countries to improve their business environment and secure sustainable economic development).

Moreover, the enhanced GTI economic cooperation helps to improve political relations and stability in the Northeast Asian Region, which has been marked in the past by the scars of the Cold War, national division, international power struggle and conflicts, and still remains not the most stable one. To ensure the stable and sound development in the future, all countries of the region should strengthen their joint efforts and reinforce cooperative mechanisms. In today's globalizing world, the challenges which we are facing—such as climate change, financial crisis, food and energy security, natural deceases—could be effectively treated only by joint efforts. If all six NEA countries (China, ROK, Mongolia, Russia, DPRK, Japan) would be involved in the one integrative framework, this would provide the best cooperation platform and mutual benefits for all countries of the region.

I GTI Progress Achieved

During the 15 years of its existence GTI has achieved a remarkable progress in strengthening regional cooperation in NEA and in Tumen region in particular.

One of the most important steps in the promotion of the GTI cooperation was done in 2005 in Changchun, at the 8th meeting of the GTI Consultative Commission. The governments agreed then to extend the originally concluded agreements for another 10 years and adopted so called Changchun Agreements in which they committed to take the full ownership of the Greater Tumen Initiative through increased contribution of financial and human resources—with the continuous support by UNDP. The meeting adopted the GTI Strategic Action Plan 2006-2015, identifying four priority sectors for joint cooperation: transport, energy, tourism and investment, with environment as a cross-cutting theme.

The 9th meeting of the GTI Consultative Commission was successfully held in 2007 in Vladivostok, Russia, marked with another progress in regional cooperation. This meeting proved to be a turning-point, demonstrating a shift to a more pragmatic approach to cooperation, focusing on development in real sectors of economy. A number of "GTI projects" were earmarked by the member countries for joint realization. The GTI institutional structures—the Energy Board, the Tourism Board and the Environment Board—were created to boost regional cooperation in key sectors of economy. With the strong support provided by the UN Office for Partnership and UNDP, the GTI Business Advisory Council (BAC) was established to serve as an effective private-public partnership mechanism for economic cooperation in the region.

The 10th meeting of the GTI Consultative Commission, the 2nd Investment Forum and the 3rd BAC meeting were successfully concluded in March 2009 in Ulaanbaatar, Mongolia. The Ulaanbaatar Declaration, adopted by the meeting, summarized the main discussions and results achieved. This meeting demonstrated the progress in regional cooperation among GTI countries and resulted in a number of concrete decisions.

A new institutional structure—the GTI Transport Board—was established with the purpose of developing a proper transport infrastructure and a logistical network to support economic cooperation among GTI countries. The first meeting of GTI transport Board will take place later this year.

For the purposes of technical procedural facilitation of regional trade among the GTI countries, the participants expressed their interest in the establishment of the Trade Facilitation Committee, aimed at the promotion of the regional trade and elimination of artificial trade barriers.

The GTI cooperation is actively supported not only by GTI central governments, but also by regional and local authorities, NGOs and business community. During the 10th CC meeting, a joint session with the GTI Business Advisory Council and the 3rd meeting of BAC were held, which laid a solid foundation for strengthening the public-private dialogue in Northeast Asia.

At the current stage, the GTI member governments pay more attention to practical economic integration and continue to cooperate in the realization of so called "GTI Projects" (approved by the Consultative Commission for joint realization). The GTI projects include NEA Ferry Route (Sokcho-Niigata-Zarubino-Hunchun), Modernization of Zarubino Port in Russia, Tumen River water protection, Mongolia-China Railway Construction, Capacity Building in the Energy sector, Resumption of Hunchun-Makhalino railway, Road & Harbor project on China-DPRK border, Multi-destination tourism development and others.

The member countries are undertaken concrete steps for the realization of these projects and to attract more foreign investment. As tasked by GTI Consultative Commission, the Tumen Secretariat is continuously undertaking activities to promote and brand these projects.

▌The Way Forward

In order to ensure further successful development of the Northeast Asia region, the joint efforts of NEA countries and international organizations are needed. This task shall include the strengthening of multilateral cooperative mechanisms in NEA with its legal basis and financial instruments; providing more strong high-level political support; developing of partnerships, the advocacy of the region and its potential; the simplification of the procedures of cross-border goods flows; improvement of business environment etc.

The NEA countries are showing in the last years the growing interest for joint cooperation. There are numerous evidences of high-level attention of the GTI countries to the regional affairs: the Federal Program on Promotion of Far East and Siberia, adopted by the Russian government; the forthcoming (2012) APEC meeting in Vladivostok; the Chinese Central government Programme of Revitalization of the Northeast Industrial provinces and the approval of Border Development Zone in the Tumen River Delta; the starting negotiations between ROK and DPRK on creation of first joint venture in food industry in the Rason zone; the forthcoming construction of Mongolian transit railways; the development of NEA Ferry Route and the discussion on the construction of undersea tunnels between ROK, Japan and China —all this provide the unique opportunities for boosting trade, investment and sustainable development in the region.

The facilitation of economic integration in the region is per se a very important task, but the strengthening of good neighborhood and mutual understanding among the peoples should not be disregarded as of less important. From this point of view much more is needed to be done to promote better understanding and confidence between people of NEA countries. The sustainable development of the region is not only the inter-governmental deal, but also the matter of social responsibility for business, NGOs and academic institutions. There is a high need for creation of special Funds for NEA cooperation, which could deal with common education, communication and cultural activities in the Northeast Asia. In this regard the joint events organized by GTI together with other partners, such as UN Office for Partnerships, UN World Tourism Organization, NEAR, Jeju Peace Institute and others play a very important role in the promotion of the peaceful and sustainable development in NEA, and we are looking forward to strengthen and develop our cooperation and partnership in the coming period.

---

* JPI PeaceNet No.3 published on February 26, 2010 in English

Breaking History's Spell on Sino-American Relations

WANG Fan
Institute of International Relations
China Foreign Affairs University

At the beginning of 2010, tensions began to build in Sino-American relations. The setback is related to American President Barack Obama's positions on Taiwan and Tibet. After announcing his decision to sell arms to Taiwan, Obama declared that he would meet Dalai Lama. By taking such stances on issues of vital interest to China, Obama faces strong objections from the Chinese side. His decisions undermined the bilateral relations, which showed signs of progress in the year 2009.

Back in 2009, many observers had very high expectations of Sino-American relations under the Obama administration. The year saw the 30th anniversary of the establishment of diplomatic relations between the two countries. As the first U.S. president to pay a state visit to China during his first year in office, Obama signed the Sino-U.S. Joint Statement with President Hu Jintao, in which the two countries pledged to work together on a wide range of issues. The Joint Statement confirmed the two sides' commitment to "build a partnership to address common challenges."

Scholars like to put new labels on Sino-American relations. On the optimistic side, many U.S. scholars preached the G2 idea, arguing that together the United States and China can rule the world. On the pessimistic side, we have international relations scholars issuing warning of a "new cold war." These scholars fear that relations between China and the United States will be as confrontational as those between the United States and the Soviet Union in the Cold War era.

Neither G2 nor the new cold war reveals the true nature of Sino-American relations. China and the United States are not on a collision course with each other. In the past thirty years, the bilateral relations are becoming more interdependent. China has explored all sorts of ways to strengthen the bilateral relations. Persistent Chinese efforts laid a firm foundation for the sound development of the relations. The two countries have built up many mechanisms of cooperation. Positive developments in recent years include the hotline between the top leaders, the China-U.S. Strategic and

Economic Dialogue and military-to-military exchanges between the two countries.

Among all the catchwords on Sino-American relations, the best phrase to characterize the relations is complex interdependence. The competitive interdependent relations between China and the United States are sensitive, fragile and complicated. The academic world is divided into realists and liberalists. Such dichotomy makes it impossible to explain the complicated relations through a single theoretical lens. Competitions between the United States and China may increase the risks of conflicts. At the same time, frequent interactions may increase bilateral cooperation, which reinforces the interdependence between the two countries.

Looking back at the twists and turns in Sino-American relations in the past 30 years, it is clear that what is plaguing the bilateral relations right now are still the old questions. In the past decades, under every president of the United States, the "three Ts," namely, Taiwan, Tibet and Trade frequently led to frictions between China and the United States.

Reflecting on the legacies of the past, Chinese statesman Deng Xiaoping once made a brilliant comment on Sino-American relations, "The relations between the two countries can not become too good, nor can it go too bad." It seems as if Deng's comment was a spell cast by history on the bilateral relations. Over all these years the two countries have never managed to come out of this pattern of bilateral relations.

Now is the time for us to think of ingenious ways to break the spell. The best solution for the relations between the two countries to move forward is to change the mindset of the past and take a global and strategic perspective. I present a package of four "go beyonds" to solve the dilemma.

First of all, we should go beyond polarity thinking. The concepts of bipolarity and multi-polarity treat nation states as the only players in the international system. Such an idea is the byproduct of power politics. It ignores how different factors interact with each other in international affairs and downgrades the power and influence of non-state actors. China and the United States should lead the cooperation between players at different levels of international community and play a more proactive role in global governance.

Secondly, we should go beyond differences of political systems and values. Different political systems will still coexist and compete for a long period of time. Some developing countries and newly emergent developed countries have made great accomplishments through their unique models of development.

These achievements show that countries should choose a development strategy suitable for their own characteristics. There is no universal political system in the world for all countries to copy. Efforts to explore different modes of development not only offer valuable experiences for future generalizations but also show the creativity of mankind.

Thirdly, we should go beyond regional cooperation and seek global cooperation. In the Asia-Pacific region, Sino-American cooperation on the North Korean nuclear issue sets a good example on solving regional hotspots. To tackle global issues like energy, climate change, terrorism and nonproliferation, cooperation between the two countries is indispensable. These new issues add to the width and depth of the bilateral relations. China does not seek to rule the world with the United States. As a permanent member of the United Nations, it will play an active and constructive role on regional issues. In this sense, cooperation between the United States and China are not limited to any region.

Fourthly, we should go beyond power politics. Power politics reflects some reality of international politics, such a way of thinking is the greatest obstacle in Sino-American relations. Under such a mentality, struggles and conflicts are inevitable. In an age of globalization, the narrow power politics perspective fails to offer us the best solutions to the current problems in the bilateral relations. To change such a way of thinking, efforts from the Chinese side alone are not enough. The two sides should work together to build up mutual trust and push forward the relations.

---

* JPI PeaceNet No.5 published on March 9, 2010 in English

Taiwanese Contentious Politics and Controversies over Taiwan-China ECFA

Hsin-Huang Michael HSIAO
Institute of Sociology
Academia Sinica

After almost one year of political disputes and public mistrust, Taiwan's President Ma Ying-jeou finally was forced to face all doubts in a press conference on Feb. 9, 2010, trying to defend the reasons why his KMT government has tried so hard to push for signing an Economic Cooperation Framework Agreement (ECFA) with China. Ma argued that such free trade pack with China will greatly help Taiwanese people to do business in China without tariff, and more importantly, once ECFA is signed, barriers to Taiwan's effort to negotiate FTAs with ASEAN countries would be reduced. He, however, admitted the ECFA would bring both opportunities and risks to Taiwan, and his administration would take measures to minimize any damage. A compensation fund of US $3 billions would be established to this need, and no agricultural products could be imported into Taiwanese market as the impacts would be devastating. Ma also promised to keep the negotiation process with China transparent, but refused to be monitored by a proposed bi-partisan legislative task force as requested by the opposition DDP. In responding to a question raised in the press conference, Ma further ensured no "political language" such as "peaceful unification" or "one country, two systems" will appear in the pack, as he wants to keep ECFA economic rather than political.

Accompanied Ma was Vice President Siew, Premiere Wu, Minister of Economic Affairs Shih, and Minister of Mainland Affairs Lai, none of them offered additional explanation or comment. In the past twelve months, all of these high ranking officials and their offices have apparently failed to convey and convince the Taiwanese public concerning ECFA. Did President Ma really successfully clear all doubts and the opposition DPP would buy it and the public would believe it? The answer is unfortunately no.

▌ Political Disputes Continued

Right after Ma's press conference, DPP Chairwoman Tsai Ing-wen expressed disappointment and criticized Ma for failing to allay public anxiety and suspicion that ECFA would adversely affect Taiwan. Ma did not specify what "risks" were and elaborate which industries and workers would be hurt under the deal and how they could be helped by the government. It is estimated that Taiwan's unemployment rate would rise to 7% to 8%, and many small and medium enterprises would be closed, and the agricultural sector would seriously be damaged. Furthermore, the most obvious economic risk would be the total dependence of Taiwan economy on China, given the fact that China is already the biggest trading and investment partner for Taiwan. Presently, 70% of Taiwanese investment goes to China and 40% of Taiwanese export is into China. Once the pack is signed, Taiwan will be completely controlled by the so-called "One China Market," a prelude to the "One China politics" as many critics in Taiwan have openly warned and feared. To many political critics in Taiwan, the Taiwan-China economic and trade links can not be treated as an economic matter. One simple fact is that China can not be regarded as a regular and normal trading partner, as China has an open political agenda to annex Taiwan. The sovereignty of Taiwan will be the most serious cost of all in signing ECFA. To opposition parties and many concerned citizens in Taiwan, sovereignty and national integrity of Taiwan is the central issue of political disputes surrounding ECFA controversy. As DPP Chairwoman Tsai warns, China would definitely ask Taiwan for reciprocate on political issues. In fact, Wang Yi, Director of Taiwan Affairs in PRC's Department of State Affairs already stated that once ECFA is signed, no more economic issues remain to be resolved, and political negotiations should follow. With all the political questions raised by opposition parties and critics remain unanswered, Ma's guarantee to have no "political languages" in ECFA really does not help much at all.

▌ Public Suspicion Unsolved

Since last Feb. when Ma began to push for further economic integration pack with China, the first wave of public debate and confusion followed immediately. The overwhelming social reaction were doubt and uncertainty about what social and economic impacts such integration might bring about to Taiwan's small and medium business, workers, farmers, and the general social cohesion. The more the government tried to hard sell the pack by one-sided promotion of the benefits with deliberate avoidance of the costs resulting from signing it, the more suspicious the general publics have become. As early as March 2009, a poll conducted by DPP showed that 45% did not know about such pack (whatever its name actually was), 49% concerned about a further economic cooperation might cause Taiwan's over dependence on China and even affect Taiwan's autonomy, 57%

disagreed with the governmental line that without strengthening economic links, Taiwan would be excluded and isolated from international economic and trade relations, and 71% worried about the dumping of cheap goods and agricultural products from China and the worsening jobless problems once the cross-straits economic links furthered.

At that time, the public already expressed clear concern about the political consequences of the pack with China, though Ma government always refrained from mentioning about the inevitable political impacts. Because of its evident political nature, 78% of the public claimed that the government should first make a consensus with the opposition parties, 89% demanded a prior discussion and monitor in the legislative body, 64% even advocated for a referendum since the pack with China could involve national sovereignty issue, 80% objected any economic cooperation agreement signed under the "One China principle" as insisted by PRC all along. Finally, more than a half of Taiwanese public (54%) expressed no confidence on Ma government's ability to protect Taiwan's interest in the cross-straits negotiation.

In another poll by Global View Magazine in December 2009, it was still found that nearly a half of Taiwan citizens (49%) did not believe that Ma administration could really protect the public interest and minimize the negative impacts of ECFA.

The most recent poll released by DPP further revealed that as high as 68% of the public gave no confidence to the existing legislative body to effectively monitor the administrative branch's China policy, and 74% supported to establish a separate bi-partisan task force in monitoring the ECFA negotiation. Therefore, it is clear that after a full year of policy promotion and Public persuasion, the Ma government still failed to convince the Taiwanese citizens concerning the proposed ECFA signing with China. And that was why, in the press conference on Feb.9, Ma for the first time openly stated that the on-going negotiation has no fixed time table. Premier Wu even declared that if no complete public confidence, ECFA negotiation can be halted anytime.

▌Class Conflict Increased

One very serious ECFA social impact would be the increasing social class conflict that Ma government dared not even to mention about it. At first, advocate for any forms of cross-straits economic cooperation agreements came from those big businessmen and capitalists who have vested interests in China trade and investment as soon as Ma got elected as the President of Taiwan in March 2008. One year later, Ma announced his Taiwan-China economic pack first in the name of CECA (Comprehensive Economic Cooperation Agreement) in Feb. of 2009, later it was changed to ECFA (Economic Cooperation Framework Agreement) in April 2009. Regardless of the name of the cross-straits economic pack, the nature has always been to enhance the Taiwan-China economic integration in order to protect and consolidate the vested interests of those pro-China Taiwanese capitalists and business sectors. As pointed out earlier, many political and social critics (from social movement organizations of labor and farmers) have openly worried that such further economic integration would inevitably cause many social problems such as the closure small and medium business, worsening unemployment for blue collar workers, forced jobless for farmers, and displacement of many managerial and professional middle class, and even overall regression of salary levels for Taiwan's job market. From the social and public view, ECFA was definitely for the rich and at the expense of the poor. Some media even coined the alarming term of "new class struggles" to imply the social consequence of ECFA.

Concluding Word

In conclusion, ECFA as advocated by the "unholy alliance" of KMT's Ma government, Taiwanese big business interests, and China has now faced a strong resistance from Taiwan's political opposition parties, general public, and civil society advocates. Two persistent warnings from the critics are quite straightforward.

The first is that if ECFA can really foster peace between Taiwan and China by a further economic cooperation, then it must not be obtained at the cost of Taiwan's national sovereignty. The second is that if ECFA can really bring in more fortune to Taiwan, it must not be achieved at the sacrifice of the middle class, workers and farmers.

.

---

* JPI PeaceNet No.6 published on March 17, 2010 in English

A Chinese Perspective on Inter-strait Relationship concerning ECFA

Dingli SHEN
Fudan University

Though mainland China and Taiwan remain non-unified for over six decades, the two sides have been engaging economically since late 1980s. Currently, they are negotiating an Economic Cooperation Framework Agreement (ECFA), which is likely to be signed this May or June.

To what ECFA has been revealed, it will entail three components: free-trade across the Taiwan Strait; bilateral investment protection; and enhancing the protection of intellectual property rights. Given ever increasing two-way trade between the mainland and Taiwan (the mainland is now Taiwan's #1 trade partner), it is crucial that the two sides talk and cut a deal, assuring their smooth economic cooperation which will improve the likelihood of peace and security across the strait.

For decades, the political distrust between the mainland and Taiwan and their non-unification reality has presented a perennial challenge to the peace and stability in Northeast Asia. Since 1990s, successive Taiwan leadership has repeatedly voiced that "Taiwan is a sovereign country" which has been vehemently criticized by Beijing. The United Nations and most countries in the world do not accept Taiwan's pro-independence claim.

In the meantime, the inter-strait economic interaction has been steadily intensifying. Thus far, Taiwan has invested in the mainland for some USD 70-80B, and it has enjoyed an annual sizeable trade surplus. In order to protect its job, agriculture and some relatively weak industries, Taiwan has regulated to ban the importation of some 2,200 items from the mainland. Also, it has refused the mainland's investment on and labors to enter Taiwan.

It is widely believed that the mainland has strategically tolerated such unfair trade and economic relations with Taiwan—by rendering more benefits to Taiwan, Beijing undercuts the push of Taiwan independence movement. Though such independence push is still around, it is largely understood that the inter-strait relations could be even worse if Taiwan has less stakes in its trade with the mainland.

Reportedly, the ECFA will offer Taiwan more benefits. Theoretically, any cross-strait arrangement has to be equally beneficial. But the reality is that Taiwan has refused to accepted 873 agricultural items as well as some 1,300 industrial items of importation from the mainland, in sharp contrast with the mainland that imposes no such restrictions on Taiwan at all. It is understood that after signing the ECFA, the Taiwan authority will retain its current agricultural restriction in importation and will not lower its tax on those some 1,400 agricultural items that are open to import from the mainland. However, given ECFA, the mainland is supposed to either implement tariff-free policy or further lower importation tax to unilaterally "yield" interests to Taiwan. Since their ECFA is virtually unsymmetrical, Taiwan is expected to save US$9B from reduced tariff while the mainland could only save US$1.3B. Also, it is expected that the ECFA could help create some 260,000 jobs in Taiwan, and help its GDP to increase by 1.65-1.72%.

Despite the vocal quest for "mutual interest," the mainland has determined to yield interests to Taiwan as its sincerity toward Taiwan people. In short term, the mainland seems to accept some unequal agreement to impair its own economic interest; but in long run, the mainland could shape Taiwan government to work with the mainland in a more stable and dependent manner, reducing the political and security risk of an across-strait confrontation, even if the agenda of unification is still out of any realistic picture.

In agreement term, the two sides will be obliged unequally, favoring Taiwan side. Given the size of the mainland economy, China's Guangdong and Shanghai and other provinces will overtake Taiwan's economy successively. Beijing has the strength and confidence to make its economic concession to buy institutional peace in this part of the world. In the meantime, it may expect that over time Taiwan will relax its discriminatory trade policy toward the mainland after reaping its "initial harvest" through the ECFA. The mainland would demand that Taiwan to eventually remove its unfair trade practice vis-à-vis Beijing.

Taiwan shall eye more beyond the ECFA. Taipei intends to build its own free-trade partnership with other East Asian nations. However, as none of the ASEAN state members have official relationship with Taiwan, Taipei has to build such partnership with Beijing's permit. Therefore, forging such an intra-China trade code-of-conduct shall be Taiwan's first step toward building its regional free-trade architecture.

Currently, the making of ECFA is within sight. Though the intra-Chinese political in-fight offers no experience for others to follow, the inter-strait economic and trade engagement does present a constructive mode of national reconciliation. On the one hand, all governments care economic and security interests, and obviously pursue the maximization of these interests. On the other hand, at a time of globalization, the flow and exchange of economic elements expedite the emergence of an all-win notion among nations and regions. The all-win strategy facilitates a give-and-take bargain, bringing various stakeholders together.

This inter-strait bargain could possibly shed lights to the reconciliation process among all Koreans. Though the inter-strait and inter-Korea issues are not exactly the same, for the difference between "One China" and "Two Koreas," they certainly bear resemblance as in both cases unification is at stake.

On the Korean Peninsula, there also exists a deep trust gulf between the North and the South. In reality, it is hard to nurture any immediate mutual political embracing, but this shall not prevent the two Koreas to engage economically constructively in the first place, as Beijing and Taipei are doing. In a similar vein, an inter-Korea incremental process of economic and trade cooperation could be envisaged to lead to a future political reconciliation among the Koreans.

---

* JPI PeaceNet No.8 published on March 30, 2010 in English

Discussion about an East Asian Community*

I Background

• Beginning of the Discussion about an East Asian Community

In the early 1990s, Malaysian Prime Minister Mohamad Mahathir proposed the establishment of the EAEG (East Asia Economic Group), predicting the need for a regional body of collaboration in connection with the worldwide trend toward regionalism, such as the progress in the EU and the signing of the NAFTA. The discussion about the need for a regional collaboration among East Asian countries was started on the occasion of the first "ASEAN+3" summit following the Asian financial crisis of 1997.

The EAVG (East Asian Vision Group) was composed under the leadership of the South Korean government to discuss how to put the idea of regional collaboration into practice. In 2001, the group presented "an East Asian Community that pursues peace, prosperity and development" as a vision for regional collaboration among "ASEAN+3."

• Reemergence of the Discussion about an East Asian Community

A new round in the discussion about regional collaboration, including the Asia-Pacific community initiative, is briskly made among East Asian countries amid the increase in the world's attention to the region as a new center for world economy. There is a movement to reinforce the East Asia Summit (EAS), which was launched in 2005 as a forum for heads of state concerning pending regional issues, as a de-facto East Asian regional collaboration mechanism participated in by ASEAN+3+3 (Australia, India and New Zealand). There are also people pointing to the need concerning how to define its relations with ASEAN+3. The ASEAN is paying attention to the tripartite summit between Korea, China and Japan held separately from the ASEAN Summit and the operation of the system of collaboration between the three countries. Meantime, South Korea needs to take part in the discussion about regional collaboration between the East Asian countries and the establishment of an East Asian Community proactively if it is to successfully push ahead with "New Asia Diplomacy" campaign that it announced lately in 2009.

▌Status of the Regional Collaboration between East Asian Countries

• ASEAN+3 / EAS

ASEAN+3, which was started in 1997, operates a total of 57 working-level bodies in 20-plus sectors, including diplomacy, supra-national crime investigation, economy, finance, high-level talks, director general-level talks, etc., in addition to the Summit. The EAS was launched by the East Asia Study Group (EASG) for research on the implementation of the vision offered by EAVG.

• Collaboration between Korea, China and Japan

The three countries have held a Summit each year since 1999 on the occasion of the ASEAN+3 meeting and sought collaboration in diverse areas. In the beginning, they focused on collaboration on economy, cultural/personnel exchanges and collaboration with ASEAN. Now, they are gradually expanding the scope of collaboration to non-traditional security needs (i.e. disaster management and marine rescue operation), problematic countries (such as North Korea concerning its nuclear program) and issues that need international collaboration (such as environment/climatic change). The collaboration council for the three countries was operated within the ASEAN+3 framework in the beginning. Recently, they started taking a more positive attitude concerning the need for talks between them aside from ASEAN+3 as highlighted in the Summits held in Fukuoka, Japan in December 2008, and in Beijing, China in October 2009.

- ARF (ASEAN Regional Forum) / APEC (Asia-Pacific Economic Cooperation)

In addition to the bodies for regional collaboration stated in the foregoing, ARF, which is a ministerial forum, serves as a regional arena for free exchange of opinions concerning politics and national security. It contributes to preventive diplomacy concerning possible disputes between countries in the regions. The number of member countries has expanded to 27 from 18, including the 6 ASEAN countries, at the time of its launch in 1994.

APEC has also served as an arena for discussion about issues related to liberalization of trade and investment. Launched in Australia in 1989 as a ministerial forum between 12 countries, it was upgraded to a Summit at the proposal of the U.S. in 1993.

• New Initiatives: Asia Pacific Community (APC) and East Asian
  Community (EAC)

Australian Prime Minister Kevin Rudd has proposed the APC
initiative, which envisions a forum of heads of state for discussion
about political, security and economic issues related to Asia and
the Pacific. The initiative is based on the view that the EAS does
not include the U.S., the APEC focuses on economic issues, and
the ARF is only a ministerial forum focusing on security issues, i.e.
there is a need for a body that comprises more member countries,
including the U.S. and discusses comprehensive agenda items.

In any discussion about the launch of a new forum for
collaboration between Asian countries, ASEAN countries stress
the ASEAN centrality. Australia is making efforts to push ahead
with its APC initiative in which ASEAN countries play a central
role to win their support.

Prime Minster Yukio Hatoyama presented a fraternity-based
East Asian Community vision as part of the diplomatic strategy
that stresses the importance of Asian countries. It is viewed as a
political idealism wishing for regional collaboration rather than a
concrete proposal for realistic steps for a regional integration.

• The U.S. Reinforcement of Regional Collaboration in Asia

The Obama Administration of the U.S. reinforces collaboration with Asia as part of its strategy stressing multipartite approaches and international collaboration in connection with the need to cope with diverse worldwide challenges.

In January 2010, U.S. State Secretary Hillary Clinton announced the following five principles for U.S. reinforcement with its regional collaboration with Asia in her speech at the East West Center in Hawaii:

1) The U.S. bilateral alliances with Japan, South Korea, Australia, Thailand, and the Philippines, a strategic dialogue with India, a strategic and economic dialogue with China, and a comprehensive partnership with Indonesia, and partnerships with newer partners like Vietnam and longstanding partners like Singapore.

2) Advancement of clear and increasingly shared objectives of regional body for collaboration: Security, economic growth, democracy and human rights.

3) Effectiveness and result-orientedness in the operation of regional body for collaboration: The formation and operation of regional groups motivated by concrete, pragmatic considerations.

4) Maintenance and enhancement of flexibility in pursuing the

results: sub-regional institutions that advance the shared interests of groups of neighbors (such as the U.S.-Japan-Australia or the Korea-U.S.-Japan) ("minilateral collaboration").

5) Need to decide, as Asia-Pacific nations, which will be the defining regional institutions: need to include all the key stakeholders, like APEC (one that is well established) and the EAS (a more recent vintage) consultation and coordination.

Considerations to be Made Concerning Regional Collaboration in East Asia

• Overlapping of the Functions between ASEAN+3 and the EAS

When the EAS was launched, there was a consensus that ASEAN+3 should be the basis for the construction of an East Asia Community, while the EAS should be utilized as an arena for discussion about matters of common strategic interest. However, some countries in the regions (such as Australia, India, New Zealand, Japan and some ASEAN countries) wished from the beginning that the EAS may function as a mechanism for substantial regional collaboration rather than as a forum for strategic dialogue, thus raising the possibility that its functions may overlap with those of ASEAN+3.

• Expansion of the EAS

There are opinions that the number of the member countries of the EAS should be increased from the current 16 (so agreed to by ASEAN foreign ministers in April 2006) to 18, including the U.S. and Russia. At the 16th ASEAN Summit held in Hanoi in April 2010, the ASEAN recommended the participation of the two countries in the EAS, as follows:

"··· We encouraged Russia and the U.S. to deepen their engagement in an evolving regional architecture, including the possibility of their involvement with the EAS through appropriate modalities, taking into account the Leaders-led, open and inclusive nature of the EAS ···." (Cited from the ASEAN Summit Chairman's statement).

• ASEAN Watch of the Reinforcement of the Collaboration between Korea, China and Japan

It appears that ASEAN countries pay attention to the ongoing movement for the reinforcement of collaboration between the three countries, including periodical Summit, apart from ASEAN+3.

❚ Conclusion

As for South Korea, it should desirably push ahead with its policy direction for regional collaboration from a perspective of deepening of the regional collaboration rather than regional integration for a given period of time. That is to say, the country needs to be ready to cope flexibly with the development of the discussion, while adopting regionalism positively and open-mindedly, rather than expressing its position on diverse discussions definitely. Meantime, the country needs to set up a new vision and strategy concerning the regional integration to be able to exert leadership in the regional integration which is the ultimate aim of the regional collaboration.

* JPI PeaccNct No.11 published on May 18, 2010 in Korean

* This article is based on what was presented at the JPI Policy Forum on April 10, 2010, attended by AHN Seong-Doo from the MOFAT (Deputy Director-General of Bureau of South Asian And Pacific Affairs), JPI President HAN Tae-Kyu, and JPI research fellows.

Change of China's "Next Generation" Strategy for Territorial Dispute Resolution with Japan

SON Ki-Seop
Pusan University of Foreign Studies

The Chinese government's recent hard-line stance in a territorial dispute with Japan in the East China Sea served as an occasion for informing the international community of a change in its attitude concerning a territorial dispute summarized as "it can wait until the next generations" that the country has maintained cautiously.

The Senkaku/Diaoyutai Islands are a group of uninhabited islands comprised of 5 small islets and 3 submerged rocks. Japan has exercised effective control over it since the U.S. returned it to Japan, along with Okinawa in 1972, after the Pacific War. Geographically, they are located 420km to the west of Okinawa and 185km to the north of Taiwan. After a patrol boat of the

Japan Coast Guard detained a Chinese civilian ship on charges of intruding into the Japanese territorial wates on September 7, the development of the event concerning the territorial dispute over the Senkaku/Diaoyutai Islands surprised watchers and caused a diplomatic ripple, as it was quite different from the past practices. It was never expected that the Chinese government took such a hard-line stance concerning a civilian ship caught in the act of illegal fishing in another country's territorial waters, although Japan released the 14 crew members except for the captain.

The Chinese government pressurized Japan from all directions. The Chinese Foreign Ministry asked the Japanese ambassador to China to come to his office several times and asked for immediate, unconditional release of the captain of the civilian ship. On September 21, Chinese Prime Minister Wen Jiabao, who was visiting the U.S. to attend the UN General Assembly, said that his country would take a strong countermeasure, if Japan did not release the captain immediately. In the days following, the Chinese government speedily took a series of retaliatory measures, including the stoppage of tourist exchanges with Japan, tax investigation into some Japanese businesses in China, hinting about the country's development of the Chunxiao gas field alone, arresting four Japanese tourists on a charge of illegally photographing a military facility in the Hebei Province, and banning the export of rare earth elements used in the production of hi-tech hybrid cars and household appliances to Japan. Rare earth elements, which are called the vitamins of the industry, are indispensable materials in the production of hi-tech items, such as motors for hybrid cars and electric cars, environmentally-friendly household appliances, optical magnetic discs, laser equipment used in metal processing and medical equipment. China accounts for 97% of the world's production of rare earth elements. Japan entirely relied on the import from China for its needs. Thus, the Japanese business circles expressed deep concerns.

Finally, the Japanese government gave in and released Captain Zhan Qixiong on the afternoon of September 24, experiencing a diplomatic humiliation. With it, the 2-week-long squabble over a case of territorial dispute over the Senkaku/Diaoyutai Islands was settled. In the beginning, the Democratic Party (DPJ) regime led by Prime Minister Kan Naoto had said that it would put the captain on trial in accordance with the law. After giving in to the Chinese government's demand, the popularity rating of the Japanese government plummeted by more than 12%. What made China take such a hard-line stance beyond the expectation of Japan and neighboring countries?

The territorial dispute between Japan and China over the Senkaku/Diaoyutai Islands has deep historical roots. Japan insists that it has exercised effective control over the Senkaku/Diaoyutai Islands since it incorporated the islands into its territory under the legal principle of terra nullius (a land belonging to no-one) in 1895 and territorial dispute concerning them does not exist. As for China and Taiwan, they insist that the islands were originally Chinese territory and Japan took it away illegally. In 1992, the Chinese government enacted the Territorial Sea Act, announcing the islands as its territory. The Senkaku/Diaoyutai Islands came to draw attention internationally after the UN Economic Commission for Asia & the Far East (ECAFE) surveyed the area and reported the possibility of the availability of ample petroleum resources in the area in October 1968. In the ensuing period, even Taiwan and Hong Kong claimed their sovereignty over the islands. In the 1970s, China and Japan did not want to have the territorial dispute stand in the way of the forthcoming normalization of diplomatic relations and the Treaty of Peace and Friendship between them. Following the signing of the Treaty of Peace and Friendship between the two countries in 1978, the territorial sea dispute submerged under the surface. In the 1990s, the dispute came to the surface again and the issue, along with the conflict over the marine resources in the East China Sea, became a crucial pending diplomatic issue in or about 2004.

At the time of signing the Treaty of Peace and Friendship in 1978, Deng Xiaoping of China and Prime Minister Takeo Fukuda of Japan compromised on the Senkaku/Diaoyutai Islands issue, agreeing to leave it to the following generations ("Tana-age" in Japanese). Deng Xiaoping took a step back and recognized Japan's effective control over the islands. It is clear that the Chinese government put more importance on collaboration with Japan through the signing of the Treaty of Peace and Friendship than on the settlement of the territorial dispute. China strongly wished to accomplish the following objectives in cooperation with Japan: Consent to the anti-hegemony provision, expansion of economic collaboration in the private sector and stronger inter-governmental economic collaboration through the signing of the treaty. Actually, Japan agreed to provide a yen-based loan amounting to $1.5 billion to China in 1979. The Chinese government appeared to judge that it would be in its interest to defer the solution of the issues of the Senkaku/Diaoyutai Islands and the continental shelf until the following generations, just pointing out that a diplomatic conflict existed between the two countries, in consideration of the fact that Japan had exercised effective control over them.

During the 1980s, the territorial dispute stayed under the surface amidst the close political and diplomatic collaboration between the U.S., China and Japan. China and Japan maintained very close relations following Chinese General Secretary Hu Yaobang's visit to Japan in 1984 during the Yasuhiro Nakasone-led regime. The Japanese showed "China fever" on several occasions, i.e. in 1978 and 1984. In the period between the end of the 1970s and the

Tiananmen Incident in 1989, the territorial dispute did not rise to the surface under such circumstances.

However, the strategy that "it can wait until the next generations" concerning the territorial dispute started changing in the 1990s, with China's emergence as a world power. The dispute finally rose to the surface with the inauguration of Chinese President Hu Jintao, Deng Xiaping's next generation, in the 2000s. Under the leadership of Hu Jintao, the Chinese government started taking the following positions concerning the dispute over the Senkaku/ Diaoyutai Islands and the marine resources in the East China Sea.

First, in February 1992, the Chinese government enacted the Territorial Sea Act, which claims its exclusive sovereignty over the islands and other areas in dispute. It also ratified the UN Convention on the Law of the Sea in 1996. Thus, China and Japan came to be engaged in an acute confrontation with each other concerning the delineation of the EEZ and continental shelf in the East China Sea and the sovereignty over the Senkaku/ Diaoyutai Islands. Following the enactment of the Territorial Sea Act, the Chinese government's attitude was a far cry from that in the past. It started claiming its exclusive sovereignty over the Senkaku/Diaoyutai Islands. It also pushed ahead with a systematization of its marine policies in the 1990s and thereafter, drawing up comprehensive marine policy documents, including the policy concerning the Senkaku/Diaoyutai Islands. The leading ones among the documents are: the Nationwide Marine Development Plan jointly compiled (in May 1995) by the State Planning Commission, the State Marine Bureau (國家海洋局) and the National Science Council; the Overview of the State Plans on the Marine Development jointly adopted (in May 2003) by the National Development and Reform Commission, the Ministry of Land Resources, and the State Marine Bureau .

Second, the Chinese government started taking a firm attitude concerning its sovereignty over the Senkaku/Diaoyutai Islands and announcing it diplomatically. When the Japanese government arrested 7 Chinese who came ashore on the Senkaku/Diaoyutai Islands in March 2004, the Chinese Foreign Ministry asked for their immediate, unconditional release, criticized the Japanese act as violation of the international laws, and reiterated the country's claim of sovereignty over the Senkaku/Diaoyutai Islands. The Security Committee of the House of Representatives of Japan unanimously passed a resolution confirming Japan's sovereignty over the islands, but Prime Minister Junichiro Koizumi settled the problem by expelling the arrested Chinese "on a broad-minded judgment that it should be settled in a way not detrimental to the bilateral relations." In February 2005, the Japanese government announced that it would manage and protect a lighthouse built by a right-wing Japanese organization on the islands. In response, the Chinese Foreign Ministry spokesperson asserted, "Diaoyutai and islets ancillary to it are inherent territory of China and any act unilaterally taken by Japan concerning them is illegal and invalid."

The Chinese government's attitude like that became clearer in September 2010, when the Japanese government detained the captain of a Chinese civilian ship for intruding into the area close to the Senkaku/Diaoyutai Islands. The Chinese Foreign Ministry asked the Japanese ambassador to China to come to its office several times to lodge a protest. Even after Japan's release of the captain, it asked for Japan's apology and compensation, stressing, "Diaoyutai and islets ancillary to it are inherent territory of China. All steps taken by Japan this time, including detainment and investigation of crew members of a civilian ship, are all illegal and invalid." In response, the Japanese Foreign Ministry spokesman said, "The Senkaku Islands are clearly Japanese territory both historically and from an international law perspective. The incident that occurred this time is a Chinese civilian ship engaged in obstruction of official business. We cannot accept China's request for apology and compensation, as it is totally groundless."

Third, the dispute over the marine resources in the East China Sea has intensified since about 2004. Starting in or about August 2003, China disclosed its plan for the development of the natural gas fields named Chunxiao and Danxiao close to the islands in dispute. In defiance, the Japanese government carried out a three-dimensional survey of the structure of the stratum in nearby waters in July 2004. In April 2005, the Japanese government asked China to stop its development in the said areas, announcing the result of its survey that the two gas fields are connected with the Senkaku Islands and saying that it was ready to deliver the relevant materials related to the survey to China. Seeing that China showed no response, the Japanese Ministry of Economy, Trade and Industry of Japan started the procedure for approving the right for excavation applied for by a private business. At that time, Chinese staged anti-Japan rallies in many cities nationwide. In the one-year period from May 2005, high-ranking foreign ministry officials of the two countries met five times. During the 4th (in March 2006) and 5th meeting, China agreed to discuss joint development of the islands in dispute as proposed by Japan, but the two sides made little progress. Japan expressed its concern over China's unilateral action for the development of natural gas/ oil fields in the delicate waters and the rapid increase of activities carried out by the Chinese marine survey ships and naval ships in the East China Sea, when the matter concerning the delineation of the EEZ remained unsettled.

In 2006 and thereafter, the territorial dispute between China and Japan entered a "calming-down" phase with the consent to the strategic, mutually beneficial relations made by the Chinese government led by Hu Jintao and the LDP (Liberal Democratic Party) led Japanese government. In December 2007, Prime Minister Wen Jiabao of China and his counterpart Yazoo Fukuda of Japan agreed to a joint development of the marine resources in the East China Sea. Thus, the territorial dispute between the two countries submerged under the surface again. The status continued even after the Democratic Party of Japan (DPJ) held power in September 2009.

However, the reemergence of the dispute in September 2010 shows that the agreements made by the two countries are only temporary measures taken strategically and that each of them seeks only what is in its interest. China took an attitude that it would never step back even an inch in the territorial dispute, when the DPJ regime of Japan proposed an initiative for the East Asian Community and Ichiro Ozawa, a party leader, led a large-scale delegation that paid a visit to China in a friendly gesture. It is thought that China will continue to carry out a strength-based diplomacy, raising its voice concerning the sovereignty over the islands in dispute, such as the Spratly Islands/Nansha Islands (between China and Vietnam) and the Sisha/the Paracel Islands (between China and the Philippines) in the South China Sea as well as those mentioned in the foregoing.

---

* JPI PeaceNet No.28 published on October 12, 2010 in Korean

The U.S.-Japan Alliance under the Democratic Party Regime of Japan

PARK Cheol Hee
Seoul National University

The U.S.-Japan alliance became more solid while Junichiro Koizumi led the country as Prime Minister. During the same period, the South Korea-U.S. alliance became sour under the leadership of President Roh Moo-hyun. At present (2010), the relations between South Korea/Japan with the U.S. appear to be the opposite of the situation under Roh Moo-hyun and Junichiro Koizumi. Under the leadership of President Lee Myung-bak, South Korea has developed its relations with the U.S. into the "21st Century Strategic Alliance based on comprehensive collaboration," whereas the Japan-U.S. alliance appears to be in an awkward state under the Prime Minister from the Democratic Party (DPJ).

As far as its alliance with the U.S. is concerned, Japan's problem stems from the inability of the DPJ to present a comprehensive diplomacy and national security-related blueprint after it took power from the Liberal Democratic Party (LDP). Basically, the DPJ's diplomacy and national security-related strategy was started from the negative appraisal of that of the LDP, particularly under Junichiro Koizumi, and it changed the course.

Koizumi's foreign strategy reached its prime in or about 2005, when his regime was also at its highest point. He globalized the country's alliance with the U.S. in a way that made it possible for the two countries to operate their forces' combined combat strength integratively on the basis of the strategic objectives shared through the "2+2 strategic dialogue." Koizumi laid the groundwork for his country and the U.S. to view issues from the same perspective and carry out actions together concerning a contingency in the region and for the worldwide security as well as for the defense of Japan through the division of roles and the integration of functions between the Self-Defense Force of Japan and the USFJ and full utilization of airbases in Jima and Yokota. The two countries also agreed to move the U.S. Marines from the Futenma Base in Okinawa to Henoko in Okinawa and Guam in connection with the need for flexible operation of the U.S. forces and the decrease the complaints of residents in Okinawa.

The Koizumi-led Japanese government also laid the basis for the Self-Defense Force's participation in international peacekeeping activities in addition to its role of defending the country by making international security part of the inherent function of the Japanese forces.

However, the spread of Japan's conflicts with Korea and China existed behind Japan's efforts to reinforce its alliance with the U.S. in that manner. Japan's attempt to become a permanent member the UN Security Council was faced with China's opposition and the diplomatic conflicts between the two countries heightened. As for Japan's relations with South Korea, the two countries came to be in a diplomatic struggle over the Dokdo issue in February 2005. President Roh Moo-hyun even declared "diplomatic war" with Japan. That is to say, Japan appeared to stake everything on the reinforcement of the alliance with the U.S., but did not mind souring relations with South Korea and China. The Yomiuri Shimbun referred to Koizumi as "one that turned diplomacy into a verbal brawl." As one depending on typical populist tactics, Koizumi revealed the lack of a strategy concerning the Asian countries, while depending heavily on the friendly relations with the U.S. Right before stepping down as prime minister, he and U.S. President George Bush paid a visit to Elvis Presley's hometown in Memphis, Tennessee. There, he sang "I love you, I need you." It displayed the Koizumi diplomacy symbolically.

The framework of the newly sworn-in DPJ regime was antagonism against the Koizumi diplomacy. The regime was not opposed to the country's friendly relations with the U.S., but withdrew the diplomacy that stakes everything on the U.S. It set up a guideline for maintaining "equal relations as an ally" with the U.S., which was similar to the line adopted by the Roh Moo-hyun's Administration of South Korea. In short, the new Japanese government was saying that it would not refrain from expressing complaints against the U.S., if any. And as a departure from the Koizumi diplomacy, it expressed a commitment to the reinforcement of diplomatic relations toward other East Asian countries, trying to restore friendly relations with neighboring countries and launch an East Asian community.

However, the change in course in Japan's alliance with the U.S. was not a simple thing to do. Japan and the U.S. had already agreed to the relocation of the Futenma Air Base in Okinawa. Prime Minister Yukio Hatoyama made a campaign pledge that he would do his best for the relocation of the base out of Japan. If he had stuck to his campaign pledge, it would require amendment to the agreement made with the U.S. If he had accepted the agreement already made with the U.S. for the relocation of the base to another prefecture in Okinawa, he would have to obtain the consent of the residents of the relevant prefecture and coordination between other local administrative units. However, the Hatoyama-led regime did not have the political capability to meet the requirements demanded by either option. Neither was it in a position to offer an alternative. After all, the Futenma issue served as an inhibitive factor that did harm the stability of the regime, which had set the end of May 2010 as the deadline for the settlement of the issue.

Basically, the problem stated in the foregoing paragraph stemmed from the idealistic view held by the Hatoyama regime concerning national security. It overlooked the fact that the Japan-U.S. Security Treaty could exist only through Japan's provision of bases to U.S. forces when making the campaign pledge for the relocation of the Futenma Air Base out of the country. Any consideration of reduction of U.S. forces in Okinawa required stabilization of the regional security. Such was not a realistically wise choice amid the challenge from the rapidly growing military strength of China and North Korea, which was developing nuclear weapons and frequently making trouble, including the attack on the Cheonan. Another precondition to the reduction of U.S. forces in the region would be the considerable progress in the launch of an East Asian community, which will weaken the need for the presence of U.S. forces as a guardian of the countries. However, one cannot see any sign of alleviated unease about security in the region despite the more positive security-related collaboration between countries in the region. The DPJ regime's idealistic security concept was an option hard to accept realistically. Under a circumstance in which Japan could not provide an option for the U.S. forces leaving Okinawa at Japan's request, with no Japanese local administrative unit willing to accept them, the U.S. and Japan would be sending out a message that it is necessary to reduce USFJ. In short, the DPJ regime overlooked the fact that U.S. forces in Okinawa do not exist only for the defense of Japan.

Recently, such a situation appears to be changing slightly on the occasion of the territorial dispute between Japan and China over Senkaku/Diaoyutai. Japan made a diplomatic blunder by detaining the captain of a Chinese ship on the charge of intruding into the Senkaku Islands illegally. It meant that Japan informed the world that a territorial dispute existed concerning Senkaku/Diaoyutai, despite its official position to the contrary. China pressurized Japan by asking the Japanese ambassador to come to a Chinese government office in early hours several times, putting a limit on Chinese's visit to Japan for tourism, banning the export of rare earth elements to Japan, and arresting Japanese tourists on charges of photographing a military facility.

China showed that its external strategy was changing aggressively by continuing to ask for Japan's apology although Japan surrendered and released the captain. As for China, it appears that the country has failed to note, or not minded, the fact such a hardline measure is not in its interest on a long-term basis, although it was effective on a short-term basis, in the settlement of a problem between the two countries. China's threat over the Taiwan Strait in 1996 resulted in the international community's stronger dubious stance toward it and neighboring countries' heavier dependence on the U.S. Needless to say, such an attitude taken by China over Senkaku/Diaoyutai will cause neighboring countries to be more watchful over China. China's adoption of an aggressive tactics will make neighboring countries, including Japan, turn to the U.S. as a guardian.

The current Japanese government is trying to restore its alliance with the U.S. by appointing Seiji Maehara as foreign minister, an expert on the U.S. and a realist concerning diplomatic and security matters. Following Seiji Maehara's meeting with the U.S. State Secretary Hillary Clinton, Clinton spokesman Philip Crowley later confirmed the U.S. stance, saying, "We do believe that, because the Senkaku islands are under Japanese jurisdiction, that it is covered by the US-Japan security treaty." It appears that Japan will take measures designed to restore the strategic alliance with the U.S. one after another before U.S. President Barack Obama's visit to Japan in November.

However, such a change in the course does not mean that Japan will return to the track that used to be taken by Junichiro Koizumi summarized as taking everything from the U.S. without paying attention to collaboration with other Asian countries. Japan is only trying to make a realistic choice, putting an end to the DPJ regime's excessive idealism. The leadership of DPJ is realizing that the country cannot push ahead with other diplomatic issues well if it fails to maintain a good alliance with the U.S. and it cannot emerge as a leading country in the international community without improving its relations with other Asian countries. Watchers will see how the DPJ regime concretizes its diplomacy/ security-related strategy.

---

* JPI PeaceNet No.32 published on November 9, 2010 in Korean

Is the Creation of a Multilateral Security Mechanism in Northeast Asia Inevitable?*

Steven KIM
Asia-Pacific Center for Security Studies

▌ Introduction

Ever since the end of World War II, Northeast Asia (NEA) as a sub-region has been conspicuous by the absence of multilateral institutions. Even when the comparison is limited to East Asia, Southeast Asia has far outpaced NEA in the growth of multilateral institutions both within the region of which the Association of Southeast Nations (ASEAN) is the most prominent, as well as beyond with external partners such as ASEAN Regional Forum (ARF), East Asia Summit (EAS), and ASEAN plus Three (China, Japan, and South Korea; APT). Although Northeast Asian countries including U.S. are members of some of these multilateral organizations, they lack a formal association of their own in the region to pursue their common interests.

The biggest constraint on the development of multilateralism has been the troubled relations of the countries in the region including U.S. stemming from past and ongoing conflicts over territory and history. The historical baggage and ongoing conflicts have made the countries deeply distrustful and antagonistic toward one another that, in turn, have hampered the development of mutual trust and respect so necessary for cooperation.

But, while past and present conflicts still cloud the future of multilateralism, profound changes in the external environment have created a new strategic opening in the region for multilateral cooperation. The momentous collapse of the Soviet Union and the end of the Cold War have led to normalization of diplomatic relations between former Cold War foes such as South Korea and China/Russia; increased cross-border trade and investment, and tourism and cultural exchange; and increasingly regularized meetings among heads of state and ministers of Republic of Korea (South Korea; ROK), China, and Japan; and informal and formal dialogs to enhance mutual understanding and cooperation in dealing with transnational threats.

Lastly, although the future of Six-Party Talks to resolve the

North Korean nuclear issue is uncertain at best, these talks are the most significant effort so far by the NEA countries—South Korea, U.S., Japan, China, Russia, and North Korea (Democratic People's Republic of Korea; DPRK)—to create an ad-hoc multilateral arrangement to resolve a serious security issue stemming from the development of a nuclear weapons program by North Korea. In fact, the attempt to resolve this issue through negotiations has encouraged many analysts to argue about the possibility of the Six-Party Talks evolving into a multilateral security mechanism in NEA. Therefore the prospects for multilateralism in NEA is a classic example of whether one wishes to describe the current situation optimistically as being glass "half-full" or pessimistically as being "half-empty."

▌ End of the Cold War and Its Ramifications for Enhancing Multilateralism

Although the history of troubled relations has been a major obstacle in promoting multilateralism, the dismantling of the Cold War security structure due to the collapse of communism has set in motion powerful countervailing forces encouraging greater regional cooperation in NEA. The most important change that helped to significantly reduce tensions was the normalization of diplomatic relations between former enemies. It is important to note that the reconciliation between former enemies has been a gradual process that began after the end of the Second World War. U.S. and Japan signed the San Francisco Peace Treaty in 1951 making Japan officially an independent country and a U.S. ally and, in 1965, ROK and Japan normalized their relations at the urging of the U.S. Even before the fall of the Berlin Wall in 1989, U.S. and Japan had already established diplomatic ties with China. With the collapse of the Soviet Union, ROK normalized its relationship with Russia (1991) and China (1992).

However, pockets of Cold War remained especially on the Korean peninsula. Of all the countries, only North Korea has failed to establish diplomatic ties with any of its Cold War enemies—ROK, U.S. and Japan—and, moreover, its relationship with China and Russia have been downgraded. The parties to the Korean War, moreover, are still technically at war because they have never signed a formal peace treaty. Also, the ongoing territorial dispute between Japan and Russia has prevented them from signing a peace treaty to formally bring an end to the Second World War. Although the vestiges of the Cold War have not completely disappeared, the significant normalization of relations between former enemies has enabled them to expand their political, economic, and cultural ties that, in turn, have provided further incentives for multilateral cooperation.

One of the most startling developments in Northeast Asia other than the political has been the rapid economic integration of the region that can spur greater cooperation by creating common interests. During the Cold War, ROK and Japan were closely tied economically to the U.S., as well as to each other. U.S. was an important export market that enabled Japan to fuel its post-war recovery and ROK to achieve rapid economic development and, moreover, Japanese investment and aid played a crucial role in the early stages of South Korea's economic takeoff.

But, with the end of the Cold War and accompanying rapid economic development in China, China has increasingly become a more important economic partner for both ROK and Japan than the U.S., though the two countries still maintain a significant economic relationship with the latter. China now is the biggest trading partner for both ROK and Japan and, in the case of Korea, its trade volume with China surpasses that of both Japan and U.S. combined. ROK alone has overtaken Japan and U.S. in foreign direct investment in China and establishing a manufacturing platform in China has been crucial for Korea in expanding its world market share of key export items. For China, however, its economic relationship with the U.S. remains crucial as a source of investment and technology and as its biggest export market. The growing economic ties have spurred greater interest in the region for bilateral Free Trade Agreements between ROK and China/

Japan. A ROK-U.S. FTA, which has already been signed and ratified by the Korean National Assembly, is pending approval in U.S. Congress.

The significance of the growing economic interdependency in NEA for multilateral security cooperation is that all the parties have a common interest in insuring that their economic wellbeing is not threatened or disrupted by inter-state conflict. This common interest can lead to the creation of a multilateral security mechanism (MSM) to manage conflict by encouraging the implementation of confidence-building measures, preventive diplomacy, and conflict resolution. In short, MSM enables the member countries to manage conflict through cooperation. Therefore, growing economic integration increases the need for MSM.

While political and economic developments accompanying the end of the Cold War have been conducive to greater multilateral cooperation, the security dynamics in the region present a more complicated picture in that any potential inter-state conflicts if not managed through some form of cooperative security may lead to greater insecurity for the region. Since the end of Second World War, NEA has emerged as the greatest concentration of the world's leading political, economic, and military powers. It has three permanent members of the UN Security Council, 1st, 2nd, and 3rd largest economies in the world, three nuclear powers, and even the lesser powers such as DPRK and ROK each have the fourth and sixth largest standing army in the world respectively.

Magnifying the security ramifications of the formidable distribution of capabilities and power in the region is the increasingly fluid and uncertain security environment in NEA in the post-Cold War period. The countries in East Asia are coping with the profound changes in the regional security architecture as great powers— including both rising (China) and status-quo powers (U.S.)—jockey for position to increase their relative influence and status in the Asia-Pacific region. Because NEA is home to great powers that are rising (China), asserting (Japan), and resurging (Russia) as well as a middle power aspiring to be "global Korea," with unresolved security issues (DPRK's nuclear arms program), simmering conflicts over territory and history, potent nationalism (arising from "century of humiliation" for China and ROK), and growing energy needs, they can easily fall into a security dilemma in which the effort by one country to enhance its security leads to greater insecurity for all. Therefore, escalating tensions can spiral out of control and lead to military conflict. This would have disastrous consequences for the region and the world. Given the consequences of increasing competition and worsening of the security dilemma, countries may want to create a multilateral security mechanism to institute confidence-building measures and engage in preventive diplomacy and conflict resolution—that is, manage conflict through cooperation. Thus, paradoxically the prospect of rising tensions and escalation of conflict in the region can encourage the creation of MSM.

Lastly, countries in the region are coping with the changes in the security environment caused by the emergence of transnational threats such as terrorism, piracy, environmental degradation, illicit trafficking of drugs, arms, and people, infectious disease, and climate change. These new threats are not only growing but also are diversifying rapidly due to globalization and advances in information technology. Since transnational threats by their nature cannot be effectively addressed by the efforts of any one nation, they require multilateral solutions. Therefore, it is in the interest of NEA countries to form a MSM in order to deal more effectively with transnational threats, as well as humanitarian assistance and disaster relief (HA/DR) and complex emergencies.

Even more remarkable than the increase in government to government contacts bilaterally as well multilaterally among the governments in the region has been the explosion of people to people contacts through tourism and cultural exchange. In some respects, this has had a more profound impact in changing the attitudes of the peoples of ROK, China, and Japan toward one another than the official contacts among their governments. The remarkable growth of tourism and cultural exchange, which will only accelerate in the future, has far-reaching implications for regional cooperation. It will not only enhance mutual understanding and trust between different peoples by increasing their knowledge of each other's culture and the values and beliefs they share in common, but also the development of a common identity by creating new cultural bonds. Therefore, as the countries in NEA continue to be linked together through ever more dense network of exchanges of all kinds, the countries will be more disposed to multilateral cooperation and further integration. While the creation of MSM is by no means certain in NEA, one cannot but be hopeful that the countries with vital stakes in the peace, stability, and prosperity of the region will strive to work towards a multilateral future.

* JPI PeaceNet No.33 published on November 16, 2010 in English
* The views expressed in the article are those of the author and do not represent the views of the Asia-Pacific Center for Security Studies, U.S. Department of Defense or the U.S. government.

South Korea-Russia Relations:
A Call for New Thinking

KIM Doug Joong
Kyonggi University

On September 30th 1990 in New York, South Korea and the Soviet Union agreed to establish diplomatic relations. It was the opening of a new page in the history of South Korea. At the end of the 1980s, the world was going through epochal changes. It saw the end of the Cold War, the collapse of the Berlin Wall (1989), and the unification of Germany (1990).

The situation on the Korean Peninsula was also changing rapidly. The normalization of the relations between South Korea and the Soviet Union was decisive in the following events: the entry of the two Koreas into the UN (1991), the signing of the Inter-Korea Basic Agreement (1991) and the Joint Declaration of the Denuclearization of the Korean Peninsula (1991), and the establishment of diplomatic relations between South Korea and China (1992).

Historically, we can see how significant the influence of the Soviet Union was on the Korean Peninsula through its occupation of the northern part of the peninsula in 1945, following Japan's surrender in the Pacific War, the establishment of the North Korean regime in 1948, and the start of the Korean War by the North in 1950. All of these lead us to expect that Russia will continue to play an important role in the efforts for the resolution of the problems concerning North Korea and the reunification of the two Koreas.

This year marks the 60th anniversary of the outbreak of the Korean War, which was started by the North's attack with the support of the Soviet military. The Soviet Air Force helped the Chinese ground troops engaged in the war against the UN Forces in the winter of 1950. The daily combat journal that contains records of the activities of the Soviet 64th Independent Fighter Aviation Corps at that time is available in Seoul. Many relevant articles and a book by Doug Joong Kim, entitled The Soviet Military's Participation in the Korean War have been published.

It is regretful that the South Korean government has not made sufficient efforts to set the record straight concerning the Korean

War and the history of the relations between South Korea and Russia. On the occasion of the 60th anniversary of the Korean War, it is suggested that the records concerning the Soviet Union's direct engagement in the Korean War should be made available based on the testimonies made by Soviet pilots who carried out military duties at that time. It would be a good idea to invite the pilots to South Korea so that they may have a first-hand look at how much the country has changed. Events carried out by the South Korean government on the occasion of the 60th anniversary of the Korean War in which the Soviet Air Force was directly engaged may serve for the beginning of new relations. In addition, efforts to keep an accurate record concerning the role of the Soviet troops that occupied the northern part of Korea at the end of the Pacific War, the role of the Soviet Union in the establishment of the North Korean regime, and the economic support provided to North Korea in the postwar period will help further establish relations between South Korea and Russia as well as the two Koreas based on a better understanding of the events of the time.

In order to prepare for the future, it is necessary to examine what has happened in past decades with a willingness to set right what went wrong. Only China and Russia borders the Korean Peninsula. Koreans should remember how significant an influence Russia has on the Korean Peninsula. South Korea and Russia are also connected with each other via the East Sea. As a researcher on

South Korea-Russia relations, the author would like to make the following suggestions for the development of bilateral relations.

First, it is urgently necessary to increase the number of experts on Russia. It is embarrassing that there are insufficient numbers of experts on Russia in South Korea, with the potential Russia represents in natural resources, including petroleum and natural gas. Business people point out that they can hardly find capable Koreans to carry out activities related to Russia. They point to the unbalance between Russian language or literature majors and regional study majors specializing in Russia. This author believes that many Korean students should be encouraged to study in Russia for several years and return home in connection with the need to train experts on Russia.

Secondly, the quality of those studying in Russia should be enhanced substantially. There are limited Koreans who can write articles in specialized fields or discuss relevant subjects with Russian scholars in Russian, although there has been a sharp increase in the number of Koreans studying in Russia following the establishment of diplomatic relations in 1990. Efforts to maintain a personal network of Russian acquaintances appear to remain only at an initial phase. Relevant institutions, including the National Research Foundation of Korea, should provide positive support for experts in diverse areas and to those interested in

Russia, so that they may stay in that country studying their fields of specialization and establish a personal network of collaboration with the Russian colleagues.

Thirdly, the knowledge and information concerning Russia accumulated over past decades should be compiled systematically. This author has attended many seminars held in Korea concerning the prospect of the Six-Party Talks on North Korea's nuclear program, the security of the Korean Peninsula, and the four powers surrounding the country. In most cases, there was no scholar from Russia. Nor were there Korean experts on Russia able to analyze and explain the position of Russia in its relation with Korea. It was not easy to find those deeply interested in Russia among the audience. It shows that Russia remains distant to us after the 20 years of diplomatic relations between the two countries. Compared to other area studies, the numbers of associations specializing in Russia are limited. Under such circumstances, it will not make sense to expect to see opportunities for criticism or debate between those with diverse backgrounds and opposing views. Associations, such as the National Research Foundation of Korea, which provides support for those studying in Russia, should derive a way to collect diverse views on Russia to compensate for the disadvantageous position of the country. The author remembers that the Ministry of Foreign Affairs and Trade made such efforts in the late 1990s and experts on Russia (who usually remained low-key) expressed their views positively on meetings held to discuss how to develop the bilateral relations between South Korea and Russia.

Fourthly, the importance of the Russian Embassy in South Korea should be emphasized. Since 2008, they have held parties and invited Korean scholars on Russian studies at the embassy in Seoul. The author has felt happy to witness such efforts made by the Russian embassy in order to get closer to Koreans. Here is an example. In the early 1970s, the United States Information Agency (USIA) in Seoul carried out programs for Korean students interested in enhancing their English conversation skills. Many students attending such programs developed into leaders with pro-American viewpoints in their areas of specialty. The USIA carried out such programs with a long-term view of expanding a network of pro-American people. It will be a worthwhile effort for the Russian Embassy to undertake similar actions, such as conducting programs for students studying Russian, providing texts, and audio-visual materials for them.

Lastly, it is urgently necessary to systematize exchanges and contacts between people of the two countries. The Russian President should be included in the list of heads of state that the Korean President visits at least once a year. Periodical meetings between the Korean President and the heads of state of the four powers surrounding the Korean Peninsula and regular summits between the leaders of the two Koreas will be an important way to maintain peace and stability on the Korean Peninsula. When Koreans refer to the four powers surrounding the peninsula (the U.S., Japan, China, and Russia), they put Russia last and regard it as the least important country in terms of influence. Diplomatic efforts should be made to build closer relations with Russia.

Towards the end of the 1990s, strategic partnerships were established between the U.S. and China, between the U.S. and Russia, between Japan and China, and between China and Russia. The level of exchanges and contacts between these countries is immense. South Korea needs to increase efforts get closer to Russia, as it will help the other three powers and Russia maintain balanced and stable relations in the region. For instance, in 2003, the Korean Association of Slavic Studies (in which the author served as Director of Research) decided to hold an international seminar at a university in Russia on a biennial basis. At the first meeting held in St. Petersburg, we found that it was necessary to hold such an event reciprocally among those sharing similar specialties.

After two decades of relations, we are looking back at what we have achieved. Many Russians ask Koreans not to regard their country as "an easy source of resources." That means they are looking forward to the opportunities to build ties with Koreans on matters beyond economics. The vast land of the Russian Far East (where many ethnic Koreans live) will serve as a fine supply source of grains to the two Koreas.

There are no special safety concerns when travelling in Russia or on the Trans-Siberian Railroad. Please feel free to study the language and other subjects in Russia. More Koreans traveling and making friends with people in the region of the four powers will develop future opportunities for Korea.

---

* JPI PeaceNet No.19 published on August 3, 2010 in Korean

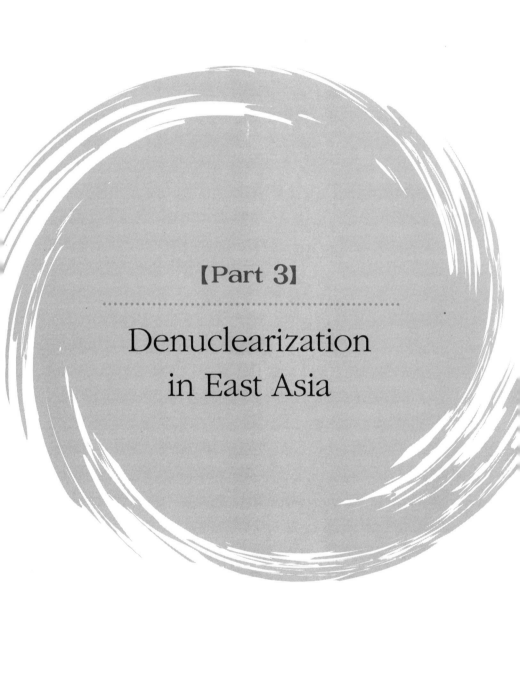

【Part 3】

Denuclearization in East Asia

Nuclear Energy Enthusiasm:
The Proliferation Implications

Sharon SQUASSONI
Center for Strategic and International Studies

Enthusiasm for nuclear energy has surged in the last few years, motivated largely by concerns about energy security and climate change. More than 27 nations since 2005 have declared they will install nuclear power for the first time. Half of these are developing countries. Some—such as Turkey, Philippines and Egypt—had abandoned programs in the past, while others, like Jordan and the United Arab Emirates, are considering nuclear power for the first time. If all these states follow through on their plans, the number of states with nuclear reactors could double.

In addition to more reactors spread more widely around the globe, this renewed interest in nuclear energy may prompt further innovations, like development of small reactors that some call "nuclear batteries," of fast reactors by advanced nuclear states and of new spent fuel recycling techniques. Several additional countries may also pursue uranium enrichment. Some of these developments could place serious pressure on the nuclear nonproliferation regime.

Thirty years ago, when an expansion in nuclear energy was similarly envisioned, the international community explored technical and institutional approaches to create a more proliferation-resistant fuel cycle. As uranium prices first dropped and then interest in nuclear energy waned, so too did the urgency of reducing the proliferation risks of expanding nuclear energy. This time, efforts to manage the nuclear fuel cycle are more urgent in light of Pakistani scientist AQ Khan's nuclear black market network, which sold uranium enrichment equipment to Iran, North Korea, and Libya, among other states, and the threat of terrorist access to nuclear material and facilities.

▌Nuclear Power: How Much Growth?

Thirty countries plus Taiwan operate nuclear power reactors (with a total capacity of about 371 Gigawatts electric, or GWe). Worldwide, nuclear energy accounts for about 15% of global electricity demand. More than half of power reactor capacity is found in the United States (25%), France, and Japan. Seven developing nations have nuclear power—Argentina, Brazil, China, India, Pakistan, South Africa, and Taiwan. Uranium ores are even more tightly concentrated, with Australia, Canada and Kazakhstan accounting for about 80% of known resources. Uranium enrichment capabilities (to make low-enriched uranium for reactor fuel) are found in 11 countries, although most of the capacity is concentrated in Russia, France, the United States, and the URENCO host states of the United Kingdom, Netherlands, and Germany. Six countries reprocess spent nuclear fuel and no country yet has opened a geologic waste repository for permanent disposal of nuclear waste.

According to the International Energy Agency, without significant policy support, nuclear energy capacity will grow less than 1% annually (or to 415 GWe) to 2030, but nuclear energy's market share would decline to 10% of electricity demand because high demand growth is anticipated overall.[1] If we assume fewer retirements of older reactors, as does the U.S. Energy Information Administration (EIA), a modest growth scenario could mean 482 GWe capacity by 2030. This would mean a stable market share for nuclear energy. A modest growth scenario sees few reactors in new nuclear states.

However, if we assume that all the states interested in nuclear power for the first time will be able to implement their optimistic

<Figure 1> Proposed "New Nuclear" States (2009)

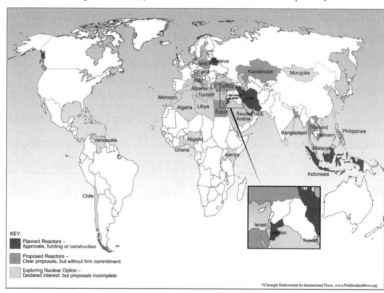

- Reprinted by permission of the Carnegie Endowment for International Peace
- Please contact CEIP at NGerami@carnegieendowment.org for the copyright

plans, nuclear capacity could double by 2030. And if global climate change concerns were to drive nuclear expansion, the capacity would reach 1 Terawatt (or almost triple the current capacity). <Figure 1> (the shaded area) shows these countries according to how far they have proceeded in their planning.

It is unlikely that all or even many of these countries will follow through in their stated timeframes for installing nuclear capacity. According to the U.S. State Department, a dozen countries are "giving serious consideration to nuclear power in the next ten years."[2] Of this dozen, several have plans to build nuclear reactors that do not now have nuclear power, including Azerbaijan, Belarus, Egypt, Indonesia, Kazakhstan, Turkey and Vietnam. Turkey is the furthest along in its plans, according to the International Atomic Energy Agency (IAEA). Nineteen countries with longer term plans, according to the State Department, include Algeria, Chile, Georgia, Ghana, Jordan, Libya, Malaysia, Morocco, Namibia, Nigeria, Bahrain, Kuwait, Oman, Saudi Arabia, Qatar, United Arab Emirates, Syria, Venezuela, and Yemen.[3]

The IAEA is providing guidance, review and support to help them build the infrastructure for nuclear energy, stressing that nuclear energy is a 100-year commitment from development to decommissioning.[4] Most developing countries would need to import reactors and, possibly, the staff to operate them. By 2020, the IAEA estimates that power plant construction could begin in eight countries, and possibly in fifteen more by 2030.[5]

Although there is growing recognition that many of these developing countries would be better served by small and medium-sized reactors (from 300 MWe to 700 MWe) because of the capacities of their electrical grids, there will be few available options for states to purchase smaller reactors in that timeframe. Both India and China have built smaller reactors (150 MWe to 500

MWe) and could become significant suppliers in the future. For now, most states will likely choose the reactors currently being marketed (between 1000 MWe and 1600 MWe).

Are these countries really ready for nuclear power? Part of the challenge for many states will be adhering to international standards and conventions that have evolved over time. <Table 1> shows the status of states that have declared an interest in nuclear power and certain nuclear safety, security, and nonproliferation commitments.

Although signing conventions is an important step toward preparing for nuclear power, the real tests of responsibility may offer less tangible evidence of compliance. For example, how will vendors, regulatory agencies and international institutions assess the maturity of nuclear safety cultures? How will states develop safety and security cultures that complement each other? Is the regulatory authority truly independent? Many of the critical requirements will take years to develop fully.

❙ Implications for Nuclear Safety, Security, and Proliferation

A global resurgence of nuclear energy could mean more than just higher numbers of reactors. Doubling the number of countries

<Table 1> States Interested in Nuclear Power: Status on Safeguards, Safety, Security and Other Conventions (as of October 2009)

Country	GWe	Target Date	Safeguards CSA	AP	Safety CNS	Security CPPNM	Waste **	Liability (Vienna Convention or CSC)
Turkey	3-4?	2014	Y	Y	Y	Y	N	N
Bangladesh	2	2015	Y	Y	Y	Y	N	N
Jordan	.5	2015	SQP	Y	N	N	N	N
Egypt	1	2015	Y	N	Y	N	N	VC
Morocco	?	2016	Y	N*	N	Y	Y	VC*
Azerbaijan	1		Y	Y	N	Y	N	N
Belarus	4	2016	Y	N*	Y	Y	Y	VC
Indonesia	6	2016	Y	Y	Y	Y	N	CSC*
Iran	6	2016	Y	N*	N	N	N	N
UAE	3	2017	SQP	N*	N	Y	N	N
Vietnam	8	2020	Y	N*	N	N	N	N
Thailand	4	2020	Y	N*	N	N	N	N
Israel	1		N	N	N	Y	N	VC*
Saudi Arabia	?		SQP	N	N	N	N	N
Oman	?		SQP	N	N	Y	N	N
Qatar	?		New SQP	N	N	Y	N	N
Bahrain	?		SQP	N	N	N	N	N
Kuwait	?		SQP	Y	Y	Y	N	N
Kazakhstan	.6	2025	Y	Y	N	Y	N	N
Nigeria	4	2025	Y	Y	Y	Y	Y	VC
Algeria	5?	2027	Y	N*	Y	Y	N	N
Ghana	1	2030	Y	Y	N	Y	N	N
Tunisia	.5	2030	Y	N*	Y	Y	N	N
Yemen	?	2030	SQP	N	N	Y	N	N
Philippines		2050	Y	N	N	Y	N	VC, CSC*
Libya	1	2050	Y	Y	N	Y	N	N
Venezuela	4?	2050	Y	N	N	N	N	N
Malaysia		2050	Y	N*	N	N	N	N

that operate nuclear power reactors, particularly if those states are developing countries, could pose risks for nuclear safety, security, and proliferation. In particular, doubling reactor capacity could require more uranium enrichment. As advanced states move toward developing the next generation of reactors, which are likely to be fast reactors that require reprocessing of spent fuel, "new" nuclear states may opt to keep their options open. Enthusiasm for nuclear growth may outpace efforts to shape the fuel cycle to minimize the risks for nuclear safety, security, and proliferation.

To mitigate risks of nuclear accidents, considerable care will be required in new construction particularly where rapid build is envisioned (e.g., in China and India); the reactor-year frequency of core damage accidents should be lowered; and reactor vendors, suppliers, and regulators should pay special attention to cultivating a nuclear safety culture, rather than just insisting that recipient states sign relevant nuclear safety agreements.

To mitigate the risk of a major expansion to nuclear security, vendors and exporting countries should consider domestic terrorism threats in recipient states and eliminating highly enriched uranium and separated plutonium in the fuel cycle. This implies an open fuel cycle, where most new reactors would be light water-moderated, low-enriched-uranium-fuelled reactors. Fuel leasing arrangements, agreements to foreswear enrichment and reprocessing, or cradle-to-grave nuclear fuel supply complete the picture.

These steps would also help mitigate nuclear proliferation risks but additional measures would be needed to reduce the potential for state diversions of weapons-usable material. Supplier states should make the strengthened safeguards protocol—the so-called Additional Protocol—the new threshold for nuclear supply and seriously explore multilateralization of sensitive fuel cycle facilities. It would not be enough to advocate that new enrichment or reprocessing facilities have multilateral ownership or operation—the approach would have to apply to all existing and future facilities in order to be nondiscriminatory. Using a future treaty, such as the Fissile Material Production Cutoff Treaty, to make such restrictions legally binding could be useful. If no country is producing fissile material for nuclear weapons, do there need to be national facilities? Finally, nuclear electricity needs to be promoted as just another way to boil water, not as a prestigious endeavor that requires high-level diplomacy and accords advanced industrial level status. Stripping away the prestige attached to nuclear energy could help mitigate states' pursuit of nuclear energy to develop latent military capabilities. Advanced states should broaden their efforts to help developing states assess all options to reduce carbon emissions, across all sectors of society, not just in electricity generation.

··

1) International Energy Agency, World Energy Outlook 2008 (Paris: OECD), p.92.

2) U.S. State Department International Security Advisory Board, "Proliferation Implications of Global Expansion of Civilian Nuclear Power," April 2008, available at www.state.gov/documents/organization/105587.pdf

3) The State Department report also included Australia in this category, but the list was prepared in 2007, before Australian elections put a Labor government in power that currently has no plans for nuclear power.

4) See IAEA, Milestones in the Development of a National Infrastructure for Nuclear Power, available at http://www-pub.iaea.org/MTCD/publications/PDF/Pub1305_web.pdf

5) Akira Omoto, Direction, Division of Nuclear Power, IAEA, briefing on "IAEA support to infrastructure building in countries considering introduction of nuclear power," 2008.

---

* JPI PeaceNet No.7 published on March 22, 2010 in English

The NPT Review Conference 2010:
Challenges and Opportunities for the U.S.

Jeffrey LEWIS
The Nuclear Strategy and Nonproliferation Initiative
The New America Foundation

President Barack Obama campaigned on a foreign policy agenda that included fundamentally transforming the role of nuclear weapons in US security policy, including a commitment to set a goal of ultimately eliminating nuclear weapons. In April 2009, just a few months into his term, the President stood before a crowd of more than one-hundred thousand people in Prague, pledging to "put an end to Cold War thinking" and to "seek the peace and security of a world without nuclear weapons."

Although the President's Nobel Prize in December was largely regarded as premature by many—including the President himself—one year after Prague, the initial results of Obama's effort to transform nuclear weapons policy are beginning to appear.

Over the course of a month, the Administration will mark the one year anniversary of Prague with a series of achievements: the signing of a so-called "New START Treaty" that commits the United States and Russian to further reductions in nuclear weapons systems, the release of a Nuclear Posture Review, and a summit of world leaders to focus on securing vulnerable nuclear materials. The string of events will culminate in May with the Review Conference of the states party to the Nuclear Nonproliferation Treaty.

The timing is in part coincidence—so-called RevCons are held only ever five years—but taken together this will have been a very unusual month. Nuclear weapons issues are seldom front-page news in the United States. Yet, as the Obama Administration approached the one-year anniversary of his speech in Prague, nuclear weapons issues have consistently dominated the headlines.

Many of the details in these agreements fall short of the soaring rhetoric of Prague. The New START Treaty is a modest effort to preserve some of the transparency provided by START while making small reductions in Russian and American nuclear weapons. The Nuclear Posture Review is essentially a status quo document that has dropped the Bush Administration's rhetorical emphasis on preemption and restored continuity with decades of US nuclear weapons policy. And although the Nuclear Security Summit resulted in a few "house gifts" for the new Administration —Ukraine agreed to convert its nuclear reactors to low enriched uranium, for instance—the impact of such summits is usually ephemeral.

Yet the details may not particularly matter. When Obama set the goal of "ending Cold War thinking," he was challenging Washington policy wonks to think about nuclear weapons in very different terms than in the past. The prevailing view in Washington has largely been that nuclear weapons are neither bad nor good. What matters is who has them and how they use them. In that view, ours are good; theirs are bad.

There has always been another view of nuclear weapons, one that sees the enormous destructive power embodied in them as a shared danger that compels even adversaries to cooperate. In this view, threats like nuclear proliferation and nuclear terrorism are every bit as important, if not more so, than traditional deterrence of deliberate attack. I believe this is much closer to the President's personal view.

None of the treaties or agreements fully embraces this vision of nuclear weapons as posing a common danger. The details of historical documents often only partially realize the transformation that set in motion. It is only in retrospect that we understand their importance. If neither the START Treaty nor the Nuclear Posture Review represents a sharp break from the past, each may nonetheless represent a turning point. Such moments can be hard to sense until the changes they set in motion play out. Yet, looking back a decade from now, I am willing to wager that it will appear that the Obama Administration spent a month discussing nuclear weapons on radically different terms than in the past and that, afterwards, there was no turning back.

This is no small feat, given the divided nature of the American political system. Although numerous polls show that Americans overwhelmingly support reductions in the role and number of US nuclear weapons, the reality is more complex. If you ask people whether they support reducing the number of nuclear weapons, support is overwhelming and bipartisan—as American as motherhood and apple pie.

Yet, that support is also very shallow. Polling conducted by Greenberg Quinlan Rosner (and commission by the Open Society Institute and the Ford Foundation) suggests that Americans are not very knowledgeable about nuclear weapons and do not see nuclear threats as a particular priority. Perhaps most important, when nuclear issues become partisan—that is to say they become associated with a particular party or politician—public consensus collapses as Americans divide into Democratic and Republican camps.

The Obama Administration, therefore, has attempted to fundamentally transform American nuclear weapons policy without allowing the debate to become polarized. This is a very difficult task, but ultimately essential. Ratification of the New START treaty in the United States Senate requires a supermajority of 67 Senators—meaning that at least 8 Republicans must agree to support the treaty. In practice this requires support of the Senator Minority Leader, which is why arms control treaties that get ratified at all, tend to get ratified with overwhelming margins. The votes on the 1988 INF, 1992 START, and 2002 Moscow Treaties were 93-5, 93-6 and 95-0.

As a result, the Administration has attempted to lower the political temperature on nuclear weapons issues by limiting the scope of the Nuclear Posture Review and the New START Treaty, while maintaining support for missile defenses and increased spending on the nuclear weapons complex. Whether this strategy will succeed or not remains to be seen, though the early signs are encouraging for ratification of the New START.

This unusual April will end with the opening of the 2010 Review

Conference (or RevCon) of the States Party to the Nuclear Nonproliferation Treaty. This gathering is held only once every five years, so the timing is somewhat fortuitous. Yet, the approach of the RevCon has also created pressure that pushed the United States to conclude its delayed Nuclear Posture Review and to complete a New START Treaty with Russia.

Much of what the Administration has done since Prague has been in service of restoring US leadership on nonproliferation issues. The United States has attempted to demonstrate that it is making good faith efforts make good on its own obligations to pursue disarmament, while also asking others to do more. Yet the "deliverables" on the Prague Agenda are constrained by the American political systems. Whether there is enough overlap between views palatable in Cairo, Illinois and Cairo, Egypt, remains to be seen. But the outcome of the RevCon will be an important and early test of whether this effort has been successful.

So far, the President has been successful when taking a turn on the world stage. When Obama went to New York to chair a special session of the United Nations Security Council on arms control and proliferation, he returned with a Security Council Resolution (UNSC 1887) that endorsed his Prague agenda.

Securing a successful result of the RevCon will not be easy. As often as not, RevCons—which operate on consensus—collapse amid acrimony and recriminations. This was the case with the 2005 RevCon, which collapsed with Washington and Tehran pointing fingers at one another. The relationship between the United States and Iran is, again, shaping up to be a major battle. Although the United States has, for the first time, offered an unconditional pledge not to use nuclear weapons against states that are members of the NPT, the pledge pointedly notes a long-standing policy that states must be in compliance with their obligations to enjoy such benefits. Statements by senior officials clearly excluded North Korea, which claims to have withdrawn from the treaty, and Iran. It remains unclear how much patience the United States will show if Iran proves an obstacle, before concludes that Tehran is bent on collapsing the RevCon, and shifts strategy from achieving a successful outcome to shifting the blame.

Nor is this the only point of tension: There are plenty of potential spoilers in 2010, including Egypt and Indonesia. The Administration has been working hard to secure the cooperation of both, but we will not know whether the effort was successful until it is over. The United States and Canada are even engaged in a ridiculous spat over Canada's proposals to move toward a Secretariat for the NPT. There are many ways the RevCon can go off track.

Yet, as in the case of the New START Treaty and the Nuclear Posture Review, a successful outcome is not necessarily one in which the states reach consensus on a document. Such documents, after all, usually only represent the appearance of a consensus, with differences papered over by careful word-smithing. The more fundamental goal for the Obama Administration will be continue to transform how we think and talk about nuclear weapons, to embrace the common danger they pose and our common interest in elimination. It will be years before we can know whether that effort has been successful.

---

* JPI PeaceNet No.9 published on April 20, 2010 in English

"A World without Nuclear Weapons" and a Nuclear Umbrella

HAN Intaek
Jeju Peace Institute

President Obama's initiative for "a world without nuclear weapons," which was no more than a slogan just one year ago, is emerging as part of the US government's nuclear policy. During the month of April, the Obama Administration undertook concerted efforts to make "a world without nuclear weapons"— it published the Nuclear Posture Review (NPR) report, which lays the foundations of US nuclear strategy for the next five to ten years, signed a new Strategic Arms Reduction Treaty (START) with Russia, and held a nuclear security summit meeting. Korea has become a significant partner of the US in realizing "a world without nuclear weapons" as it is scheduled to hold the second nuclear security summit meeting next year, following on from the one held in the US.

What will the future US nuclear umbrella for Korea be like in the "world without nuclear weapons" that could be achieved in the future?

Being an ally that has enjoyed the US nuclear umbrella for several decades, we need to carefully monitor the new US nuclear policy in order to fully understand the implications for us—and especially the implications of the nuclear umbrella.

Under the new nuclear policy of the Obama Administration, a new sense of pragmatism focused on effectively addressing new security threats after the Cold War co-exists with the ideal of halting the proliferation of nuclear weapons around the world. According to the 2010 Nuclear Posture Review report, US nuclear policy has undergone a fundamental shift from an outdated strategy based on cold-war thinking to a new strategy for reducing the role of nuclear weapons in the US's defense strategy, while the focus of US nuclear policy has been switched from the prevention of nuclear war between countries to the prevention of nuclear proliferation and nuclear terrorism. This shift in the thrust of US nuclear policy is the outcome of the aforementioned combination of idealist and pragmatic strategies.

What matters is that the Cold War is not yet over on the Korean peninsula and there still exists a possibility of a new war between the two Koreas. Fortunately, the core content of the telephone conversation between President Obama and President Myeongbak Lee held shortly before the release of the new Nuclear Posture Review report is that the new US nuclear policy for the post-cold war era will not affect the US's security commitment to South Korea, as it still provides an extended nuclear deterrence against North Korea where the cold-war situation is not yet over. This was reaffirmed by US Secretary of State Hilary Clinton.

Deterrence consists in making an enemy renounce its attack plans by threatening it with a powerful retaliation to any attack. For deterrence, especially extended deterrence, to succeed, the threat that a powerful retaliation would be made if the enemy attacks should be credible most of all, so the actual military capability required for such retaliation must exist in reality. Concern in Korea about the new Nuclear Posture Review report has been substantially alleviated following President Obama and Secretary Clinton's reaffirmation of the provision of a nuclear deterrent and a security commitment, thus helping to prevent North Korea from making any erroneous judgments by enhancing the credibility of the US's intention to retaliate against an eventual North Korean attack.

For the US's extended deterrence to be successful, it should eventually be regarded by North Korea as effective. To that end, not only the commitment of the US's political leaders but also the actual capability to support such a commitment should be satisfied. The Nuclear Posture Review report is important in that it provides a significant clue as to whether the US is equipped with the military capacity required for deterrence.

The Nuclear Posture Review report is not only a symbolic yet carefully nuanced document but also a highly technical document that requires expert knowledge on military technologies and strategies. One could possibly reach the wrong conclusion by erroneously analyzing the report without considering the differences between the roles and positions of Korea and the US and the linguistic differences between the Korean and English languages. To facilitate a more accurate understanding of the new US nuclear policy, therefore, this paper intends to study the concepts or terms that may leave room for different interpretations between Korea and the US.

▌Preemptive Attack vs. First Use

Some experts believe that the US has maintained its preemptive nuclear strike policy against North Korea, Iran and other states that are not NPT member states or which are NPT member states that do not comply with the obligations under the NPT, while having renounced its preemptive nuclear strike policy against NPT member states that do comply with the NPT obligations. This is not a correct interpretation. What the Obama Administration has disclosed in its new Nuclear Posture Review report is that it renounces nuclear first use against NPT member states without nuclear weapons that comply with the NPT obligations. Nonetheless, the US may stage a preemptive attack if any such NPT member state intends to attack the US or any of its allies as long as the US does not use nuclear weapons. Furthermore, it appears not to be impossible, theoretically speaking, that the US could stage a preventive attack against such states as long as the US does not use nuclear weapons. This is because the Obama Administration has not yet officially abandoned the preemptive strike strategy adopted by the Bush Administration.

To explain this further using North Korea as an example, nuclear first use and preemptive strike are both possible against the North under the new US nuclear policy. (And, a nuclear preventive attack has not yet been excluded although the possibility of it occurring has been reduced.) A preemptive or preventive attack against North Korea is still possible within the extent the US does not use nuclear weapons, although the US will renounce preemptive nuclear attacks against North Korea if the latter rejoins the NPT and complies with all NPT obligations. One of the important reasons why few Koreans fear that the new US nuclear policy will limit the effectiveness of the extended deterrence should be that, like the Bush Administration, the Obama Administration will maintain the nuclear first use policy and preemptive attack option against North Korea.

▌ Extended Deterrence vs. Nuclear Umbrella

Nuclear weapons are generally divided into strategic and tactical nuclear weapons based on their firing range, destructive power and usage. For example, nuclear-headed ICBMs are classified into strategic nuclear weapons, while short-range nuclear missiles are classified into tactical nuclear weapons. In providing the US extended deterrence to its allies, US nuclear weapons, especially tactical nuclear weapons, have played an important role traditionally. Meanwhile, the US drastically reduced its arsenal of tactical nuclear weapons in the 1990s. Those remaining currently are a small number of tactical nuclear weapons deployed in Europe and those stored in mainland USA.

According to the 2010 Nuclear Posture Review report, the Obama Administration will continue to reduce the number of tactical nuclear weapons while retaining the capability to deploy fighter bombers and heavy bombers equipped with tactical nuclear weapons, but it plans to retire Tomahawk missiles, which played a core role in providing an extended deterrence, especially in Asia. The Obama Administration disclosed that it will fill the blank in its military strength occasioned by the retirement of the Tomahawk missiles with strategic nuclear bombers, nuclear-headed ICBMs, SLBMs, and advanced conventional weapons.

It appears to be unnecessary for the US to use such strategic nuclear weapons as nuclear-headed ICBMs or SLBMs to deter attacks by North Korea. In the case of the Korean peninsula, or South and North Korea, where the landmass is narrow and the population is heavily concentrated, short-range nuclear missiles would cause human and physical damage comparable to that which would be caused by nuclear-headed ICBMs or SLBMs owned by the US and Russia. More importantly, it could be impossible to use strategic nuclear weapons against North Korea. For example, if a nuclear-headed ICBM explodes in North Korea, South Korea and China may suffer damage from the impact and radioactive fallout. Furthermore, China or Russia could retaliate against the US with their ICBMs if they misinterpreted the ICBMs fired by the US against North Korea as an attack against them. Such a risk also applies to the conventional Prompt Global Strike (PGS) weapons the Obama Administration plans to develop to replace nuclear weapons. Therefore, though the US and Russia may require ICBMs and SLBMs, which are strategic nuclear weapons for nuclear deterrence, it can be said that tactical nuclear weapons are still virtual strategic nuclear weapons that serve as a core deterrent against North Korea.

It seems inevitable that the nature of the US's extended deterrence for South Korea will change because of the Obama administration's decision to retire the Tomahawk missiles while continuing its reduction of tactical nuclear weapons. So far, 'extended deterrence' and the 'nuclear umbrella' have generally been used as synonyms though they cannot necessarily be treated as such. If it is unnecessary or impossible to use strategic nuclear weapons as a means of providing extended deterrence as argued in this paper, it is highly possible for the future extended deterrence to rely on conventional weapons, especially advanced conventional weapons, eventually. In that case, extended deterrence will no longer be a 'nuclear' umbrella but rather a 'conventional' umbrella. Of course, we will, from now on, have to study how extended deterrence can be provided effectively and safely with conventional weapons.

❘ Necessity for Strengthening Security Diplomacy

Under the new nuclear policy of the Obama Administration, a new sense of pragmatism designed to more effectively address new security circumstances after the end of the Cold War co-exists with an idealism aimed at realizing "a world without nuclear weapons." As a partner in the worldwide efforts to halt the proliferation of nuclear weapons and as an ally of the US, Korea needs to understand the idealism and pragmatism contained in the new US nuclear policy and also to be able to correctly understand and address the changes in and continuities of the US's nuclear policy.

Most of all, Korea needs to effectively respond accordingly by understanding that the nature of the US's extended deterrence for Korea inevitably has to be changed because of the changes in US nuclear policy.

Ultimately, Korea should not spare any efforts to actively explain our needs and persuade the US when measures are required for our security. The Congressional Commission on the Strategic Posture of the United States, a non-partisan commission organized by the US Congress, was induced to conclude that Tomahawk missiles need to be maintained as the Japanese LDP (Jiminto) administration lobbied Congress by realizing the need to keep the Tomahawk missiles mentioned above. The Japanese government's stance changed after the administration was taken over by the Democratic Party (Minshuto), which expressed its agreement to the retirement of Tomahawk missiles, saying that the request made by the Jiminto administration to the Obama administration to maintain the Tomahawk missiles was not the formal position of the Japanese government. Of course, it is not known exactly how important a variable the Minshuto administration's preference was in the Obama administration's decision to retire the Tomahawk missiles. Yet, it is noteworthy that the current Japanese government expressed its agreement to the retirement of the Tomahawk missiles when it determined they were unnecessary for Japan's security, while the previous Jiminto administration requested the US to maintain them if they judged they were necessary for Japan's security. When the Obama administration decided to retire the Tomahawk missiles, it informed only Japan in advance, excluding Korea from the advance notification. This should probably be an achievement of the active Japanese security diplomacy.

---

* JPI PeaceNet No.10 published on April 28, 2010 in Korean

A Chinese Perspective on the Nuclear Posture Review

GAO Wanglai
Institute of International Relations
China Foreign Affairs University

The Nuclear Posture Review of 2010 is a key document laying out the basic contours of the United States' nuclear policy. This seminal document on United States' defense policy shows adjustment in United States' nuclear policy in the Obama administration, and will guide United States' nuclear policy in the near future. The report leads to serious debates within China on the future shape of the United States' security strategy and China's consequent response.

Since the end of 2009, the Chinese media has been following possible adjustments and analyzing the shape of the United State's future nuclear policy. After the release of the document, all the major Chinese websites covering international affairs published updates on the news and analyzed the trends within the report. Some security experts also published comments on their interpretation of the report.

Three major adjustments were made in the Nuclear Posture Review. First of all, the United States promises it will not use nuclear weapons against non-nuclear weapons states that are party to the NPT and in compliance of its nonproliferation obligations. Secondly, the Nuclear Posture Review highlights the importance of preventing nuclear terrorism and proliferation. Thirdly, the administration is going to "reinvigorate" the U.S. nuclear complex.

Published in a period of persistent U.S. efforts on nonproliferation, the report reflects President Obama's positive stance on nuclear nonproliferation since he took office. President Obama himself has been campaigning vigorously for a nuclear free world since he was a Presidential candidate. He won the Nobel Peace Prize for his dedication to the course. His persistent efforts led to some breakthrough in international nuclear arms control in the past few months. The United States and Russia signed an important agreement on cutting their nuclear arsenal. The Nuclear Security Summit in April 2010 raised public awareness on nuclear security.

Such progress in nuclear arms control is in sharp contrast to former U.S. President Bush's policy on nuclear nonproliferation. The course of international arms control went through setbacks due to President George Bush's withdrawal from the Anti-Ballistic Missile Treaty. President Bush's preemptive strike policy was the most aggressive nuclear strategy adopted by the United States, at least in rhetoric, after the end of the Cold War.

As the most powerful country in the world, the United States surpasses other nations and enjoys a unique position in nonproliferation. As a global hegemonic power, the United States possesses the world's most advanced military technology and has the agenda setting power in international arms control. Nuclear nonproliferation is a major area in which the United States plays the leading and most decisive role. President Obama effectively used this agenda-setting power to create a good atmosphere for international nuclear nonproliferation. United States' nuclear policy is related to global strategic stability. China welcomes the progress made in the report. China has always been committed to the course of nonproliferation.

In politics, we need to distinguish rhetoric from reality. In comparison with President Obama's high profile attitude and promises since he took office, the shifts in the Nuclear Posture Review are not as significant as many people had been expecting.

For an outsider of arms control, the past few months are a climax of nuclear nonproliferation, with several important meetings and great achievements.

The limits in United States' dedication to nuclear nonproliferation are evident in two major adjustments in the Nuclear Posture Review. On the one hand, United States promises not to use nuclear weapons against non-nuclear weapon states that are parties to the NPT, the idea expresses in another sense that United States reserves the right to launch possible nuclear attack on North Korea and Iran. The document adopts a more moderate tone than President Bush's Preemptive Strike Strategy. As can be seen from the expression, the Nuclear Posture Review does not rule out the possibility to use force against North Korea and Iran.

On the other hand, the Nuclear Posture Review lays out the prospect of reinvigorating the United States' nuclear complex. The idea reflects a fundamental adjustment in United States' nuclear policy, which is evident in United States' security policy at the present time. Former United States President Eisenhower had warned the possibility for military-industrial complex to dominate domestic politics. Such a measure shows that nuclear weapons remain to be a crucial part of the United States' nuclear policy.

The limited changes in the report show the tension between

President Obama's ideal of nuclear zero and the constraints from domestic politics of the United States. The United States' foreign policy shows the personal style of political leaders. Such a change of style can be spotted from the different attitudes between President Obama and former President Bush on nuclear nonproliferation. However, if we read between the lines, the changes in substance of the United States' nuclear policy are very limited.

Right now, the United States is actively involved in developing new types of nuclear weapons. The nuclear disarmament deal with Russia ensures that the United States' nuclear weapons are updated. The deal is also beneficial to the United States as it eliminates the risks of out-of-date weapons by dismantling them and cuts their preservation expenses.

Another major change in the field is that the United States introduces more transparency in its nuclear capability. On May 3, 2010, the United States released details about its nuclear stockpile today. Since the birth of nuclear weapons, the United States has announced for the first time the number of nuclear weapons, the number has been kept secret in all the earlier United States' administrations. Chinese security experts observe the progress soberly. By announcing the number of its weapons, the United States enhances its security by demonstrating to the world it possesses the most superior technology in the world and its superiority cannot be challenged by any country.

On the issue of transparency, China believes it means two things: transparency of intentions and transparency of capabilities. In transparency of intentions, China ranks the first among the five nuclear powers in pursing a non-first use nuclear policy. In transparency of capabilities, due to its hegemonic power, the United States' exposure of its nuclear capabilities fits the United States' national interests as it constitutes effective deterrence to any potential enemy. The United States also seeks to occupy a moral high ground by this gesture and pressure China to reveal its nuclear capability, which is a bargaining chip craftily employed by the United States.

The Chinese believe that there are two types of proliferations: horizontal proliferation and vertical proliferation. Horizontal proliferation means the spread of nuclear technology from one country or region to another, leading to the proliferation of nuclear technology to more countries and regions. The United States expresses clear suspicion of this type of proliferation, singling out North Korea and Iran as targets. Vertical proliferation means the upgrading of a country's nuclear capabilities. Through development of new technology and new weapons, the United States is actively involved in nuclear technology. It is upgrading its present nuclear arsenal to a new generation. Its nuclear warheads and carriers are becoming more advanced. As a result, the United States seems to be involved in nuclear disarmament. However, its nuclear capability turns out to be upgraded. Such efforts made it possible for the United States to enjoy technological edge over all other countries in the world.

Around the same time with the publication of the Nuclear Posture Review, the United States tested a secret weapon. On April 22, the United States launched X-37B Orbital Test Vehicle. The vehicle is a major breakthrough in advanced military technology for the United States. This vehicle made it possible for the United States to enjoy a "two-hour global fight against Circle." The weapon greatly increased the United States' military deterrence capability. Such a test shows the gap between the United States' promise and its real goal. The most advanced nuclear arsenal coupled with the most powerful strike weapon like X-37B, makes the United States invincible in the world.

The new Nuclear Posture Review points out an area in which China and the United States shares common interests, in nuclear terrorism and nonproliferation. If nuclear weapons fall into the hands of terrorists or other groups with hostile intentions, the consequences will be disastrous. The two sides can work together to solve global security issues. In April 2010, President Hu Jintao attended the Nuclear Security Summit in Washington D.C. hosted by President Barack Obama. In a more interdependent world, the United States and China need each other in reducing nuclear dangers and pursuing the goal of approaching a world without nuclear weapons.

In Conclusion, in comparison with the Bush administration, the Obama administration adopts a more positive attitude towards nonproliferation, which is reflected in the latest Nuclear Posture Review. Because of the domestic restraints faced by President Obama, the United States will not change its policy seeking dominance in the world. As a result, the shifts in policy will not be translated into significant change in reality. The report lays out areas of common interests between China and the United States. The Chinese government is committed to the course of nonproliferation. It will work together with the United States to push forward the course of nuclear nonproliferation.

* JPI PeaceNet No.12 published on May 25, 2010 in English

Nuclear Disarmament:
An Australian Perspective

Rod LYON
Australian Strategic Policy Institute

Australians have been broadly welcoming of President Obama's reinvigorated nuclear policy agenda—an agenda built upon the long-term prospect of nuclear disarmament and nearer-term attempts to reduce the role of nuclear weapons in global and regional security. Both government and public are broadly in agreement with any effort that constrains the further proliferation of nuclear weapons. And in 2010, a Review year for the Non-Proliferation Treaty (NPT), that objective has special importance within the Australian political leadership.

But Australians' relationship with nuclear weapons has long been an ambiguous one. For just as Australian security would be gravely damaged by a world of high nuclear proliferation, so too the extended deterrence commitments that the US has provided to Australia under the ANZUS Treaty have traditionally included a nuclear component. Australia, like many other US allies, has been in the privileged position of both forsaking nuclear weapons as an indigenous strategic option, and having them available to underpin Australian security in crises. So Australia has been both a champion of nuclear arms control and—less publicly—a beneficiary of US extended nuclear deterrence arrangements.

In some ways, then, Australia is not so different from the US—although, of course, it does not have nuclear weapons of its own—nor from other US allies in Asia who benefit from similar arrangements. Obama's nuclear policy keeps alive that dual nuclear identity both for the US and its allies for some years yet. Obama himself admits that nuclear disarmament might not occur during his lifetime, and he's scarcely an old man. His Nuclear Posture Review accepts that nuclear deterrence will underwrite US security for the foreseeable future, and thus provides a signal that the Australian government was keen to see: a confirmation of the continuing relevance of nuclear deterrence in an era of geopolitical transformation in Asia.

So what's the future of extended nuclear deterrence as the Obama 'revolution' rolls forward? Well, in some senses, despite the soaring rhetoric of the Prague speech, it is scarcely a revolution at all. But it is the fine details of the changes in US nuclear policy that merit closer attention. There are distinct hints in the Nuclear Posture Review that Obama wants to decrease further US reliance on nuclear weapons, and that means decreasing further US allies' reliance on US nuclear weapons too. The retirement of the Tomahawk land-attack nuclear-armed cruise could be seen as a hint to maritime allies—that is, Pacific allies—in particular that they should contemplate a decreased reliance upon extended nuclear deterrence in their own strategic profiles. But the nuclear-armed Tomahawk is now a comparatively old weapon system, and the Review specifically attempts to reassure allies that extended deterrence does not, in fact, turn upon specific weapon systems but upon the entire US nuclear (and conventional) arsenal.

Whether that assurance is going to be fully satisfying to US allies remains to be seen. The NPR can be read in a variety of ways. The Review's foreshadowing of a future US nuclear doctrine that accepts the principle of the 'sole purpose' argument when conditions allow—that the sole purpose of nuclear weapons then will be to deter the use of other countries' nuclear weapons— does point to a gradual shrinkage of the US nuclear umbrella previously deployed over allies. The umbrella is not shrinking abruptly, but its shrinkage at all during an era of looming geopolitical transformation in Asia is bound to generate a degree of controversy among US allies and partners. And it is in precisely those strategic circumstances that US Asian allies will view—and read—the continued removal of specific short and medium-range nuclear weapon systems from the US arsenal over recent decades. Australia, like other US allies, will in coming years watch closely the continuing unfolding of US nuclear policies in Asia.

Two other issues merit separate attention here. The first such issue involves the non-attendance of the Australian prime minister at President Obama's Nuclear Security Summit in Washington in April this year. In a year of hectic nuclear milestones—the conclusion of the New START treaty, the publication of the Nuclear Posture Review, and the NPT Review Conference in New York—Australian Prime Minister Rudd attracted some criticism for his decision not to attend the Nuclear Security Summit. (Defence Minister John Faulkner attended instead.) But this issue is not one of particular strategic gravity: it is an election year here in Australia, and domestic issues are clearly uppermost in the mind of both the competing political parties and the Australian electorate. With President Obama having cancelled his March trip to Indonesia and Australia, but re-committed to a visit in June, for the Australian prime minister to head off to Washington in April might have made the relationship look too asymmetrical. The prime minister judged, correctly, that Australian commitment to the principles of nuclear security had never been in doubt.

A second issue that needs to be canvassed is the government's announcement of the termination of the International Commission on Nuclear Nonproliferation and Disarmament (ICNND). The Commission was set up to provide a distinct forum for a detailed consideration of the broad issues of nuclear disarmament and the specific challenges of the 2010 NPT Review Conference. Whether intentional or not, the Commission had the additional advantage of providing a degree of government separation from a wide range of recommendations and proposals: essentially, it allowed the government to play in two distinct 'spaces' — the Australian policy space and the international commission space. The resourcing of the commission and its administrative support in the Department of Foreign Affairs and Trade showed a government intent upon supporting the push for new policy proposals in the nuclear arms control and disarmament arena. But I think it was never the Australian government's intention to keep the Commission running as a long-term body.

The Commission delivered its final report, Eliminating Nuclear Threats: A Practical Agenda for Global Policymakers, in Tokyo in December last year, and the Australian government delivered its response to the report in a media release on 3 May. As that response noted, the government saw the establishment of the Commission as a demonstration that nuclear non-proliferation and disarmament issues were a high priority for the government.

Further, it saw it as an opportunity to strengthen diplomatic relations with Japan on an area of shared interests and objectives. But it pointed out that the Commission was staunchly independent, and that commissioners had been appointed on the basis of their personal capacities. Most of the Commission's analysis, action agenda and recommendations were said to be 'in step' with the government's non-proliferation and disarmament policies, although the response observed that in moving towards the goal of a world without nuclear weapons, 'the government is mindful that Australian defence policy acknowledges the value to Australia of the protection afforded by extended nuclear deterrence under the US Alliance.'

The government, however, shied away from endorsing either of the Commission's two central proposals: the proposal for the achievement of a 'minimisation point' in global nuclear weapon stocks of 2,000 warheads by 2025, and the proposal that nuclear weapon states declare that the 'sole purpose' of their nuclear weapons was to deter others from using nuclear weapons against themselves or their allies. In relation to the minimisation target, the government argued instead that it was 'more important … to create the strategic and political conditions that will encourage deep and irreversible reductions.' Similarly, it gave only qualified support to the Commission's proposal for a 'sole purpose' declaration. While the response did accept that 'Australia would be comfortable' if the US was to reach a point where it felt such a declaration were possible, it did so in the context of Obama's recent Nuclear Posture Review, which noted that work was still required to establish the conditions that would allow such a declaration.

The broad sense of the government's response to the ICNND report is clearly shaped by its judgment that the Obama administration's Nuclear Posture Review provides sufficient continuity to US nuclear policy settings that it would imprudent for Australia to get out in front of its ally on disarmament policy. It is especially attracted to that conclusion by the continuing uncertainty that surrounds Asia's own strategic future: great-power strategic relativities are shifting in Asia, and the regional security environment remains an unsettled one. There is a sense in Canberra that nuclear issues are growing in importance in Asia, just as the pressure for nuclear disarmament also returns to the forefront of public attention. Striking a sensible balance on nuclear disarmament and defence policy is a growing priority for the Australian government, as it is for many other regional countries.

---

* JPI PeaceNet No.13 published on June 1, 2010 in English

Obama's Nuclear Policy and Japan's Security

Masashi NISHIHARA
Research Institute for Peace and Security

▌Extended Nuclear Deterrence Ensures Japanese Security

On April 6 when the Obama administration released the Nuclear Posture Review and outlined the need to reduce the role of nuclear weapons in the the United States security policy, the Japanese government was pleased with it. Tokyo has been a strong advocate of complete nuclear disarmament. Every year it acts as one of the leading United Nations members who introduce to its General Assembly a resolution calling for total nuclear disarmament. President Obama's nuclear posture is a significant step toward total nuclear disarmament.

However, Japan, like the United States, is realistic. While it advocates a world free of nuclear weapons, it also sees the merit of nuclear deterrence, as long as nuclear weapons exist or are likely to be held in the hands of potential adversaries, including terrorists. Japan agrees to President Obama, who remarked at Prague in April last year that "Make no mistakes: as long as these weapons exist, we will maintain a safe, secure and effective arsenal to deter any adversary, and guarantee that defense to our allies."

By reducing the role of nuclear weapons in the U.S. security policy, it will strengthen the level of conventional deterrence. Relying on conventional deterrence may be more practical, although it may increase the possibility of war. Conventional deterrence will reduce the impact of nuclear fallout on the peninsula and the Japanese islands, if North Korea will resort to nuclear attack on the south.

Being realistic, Japan welcomes Washington's new policy of extended nuclear deterrence as well. The United States now confirms the policy of employing no first use of nuclear arms against those non-nuclear countries ("negative assurance" policy) except for those nations that do not comply with the Nuclear Non-Proliferation Treaty (NPT). The U.S. government continues to uphold the first use policy against countries like North Korea and

Iran. Japan is satisfied with this conditional first use policy.

The Nuclear Posture Review was originally planned to come out in December last year. One of the reasons for the delayed release was due to disagreements within his administration over the first use of nuclear weapons. The Review, which finally came out in April, revealed that the United States had modified the traditional first use principle. There was a speculation in Japan and elsewhere prior to the release of the Review that the United States might abandon its traditional policy of the first use. By making exception for North Korea and Iran, the U.S. posture continues to ensure the security of Japan and South Korea.

In 2008-09 Japan and Australia co-chaired the International Commission on Nuclear Non-Proliferation and Disarmament. Although it was not the official international body, it was backed by the governments concerned. The report proposed, among others, the abolishment of the first use principle. The official Japanese government position is to support the first use policy by the United States since Japan benefits from being protected by the U.S. nuclear umbrella. Thus there was discrepancy between the Evans-Kawaguchi Commission and the Japanese government. The Nuclear Posture Review took a compromised policy on the first use principle, by applying it only for exceptional cases.

Japan's Non-Nuclear Policy Should be Revised

During the Cold War years Japan's official non-nuclear policy was contradictory. On the one hand it claimed that it upheld three non-nuclear principles: not to possess nuclear arms; not to produce nuclear arms; and not to allow nuclear arms to be introduced. On the other hand, it relied upon the U.S. extended nuclear deterrence. The United States naval ships that came to Japanese ports for transit visits or passed through Japan's territorial waters might have been equipped with nuclear arms. The publicly known arrangement that reached between Tokyo and Washington back in 1960 stipulated that the introduction of nuclear weapons to Japan required "prior consultation." However, in reality, the United States never asked for prior consultation. In fact, the United States took a policy of strategic ambivalence: "neither confirm nor deny" (NCND). It did not have to seek prior consultation.

Thus those critical of the Japan-U.S. alliance, particularly anti-nuclear activists, suspected that U.S. naval ships coming to Japanese ports carried nuclear arms. However, they had no way to substantiate their suspicions, because of the U.S. policy of NCND. In fact, since 1960 the Japanese government had confidentially informed the U.S. side that it would acquiesce in American ships transiting Japan or passing through Japanese territorial waters or airspace with nuclear weapons on board. Some journalists and academics have exposed these American practices by going through U.S. archives released to the public through the Freedom of Information Act. It was only confirmed by the Hatoyama government in February this year, when the investigation committee by experts set up by Foreign Minister Katsuya Okada uncovered that the secret understanding with the United States had indeed existed.

Whether this revelation by the Japanese government was a wise act remains controversial. It is in Japan's security interest to keep its strategic security option wide by allowing the United States to apply its NCND principle to the Western Pacific. Since September 1991 the United States has removed all tactical nuclear weapons like Tomahawk missiles from all surface ships. However, it may have to redeploy them in the future, as the United States says that it will keep its short and medium-range tactical nuclear weapons in European NATO countries. In that case, one of Japan's three non-nuclear principles, namely, the principle of no introduction, if strictly applied, will hinder the U.S. decision to redeploy them in the Western Pacific.

Japan should thus revise the principle of no introduction and allow the American naval ships with nuclear arms on board to make transit visits to Japan or to pass through its territorial waters. The United States has understood all along that "no introduction" of nuclear weapons means that no nuclear weapons may be introduced into the Japanese land, not necessarily into ports and territorial waters. What may well be termed as the 2.5 nuclear principles would fit both Japanese security and the U.S. policy. This is what other Pacific allies of the United States like the Republic of Korea and Australia quietly have been practicing.

---

* JPI PeaceNet No.16 published on June 18, 2010 in English

Spring-2010: Will It Become A Turning Point on The Road to Nuclear Free World? A View from Russia

Sergey M. SMIRNOV
Center for International Studies
Maritime State University

I think that nobody would challenge the Obama administration lead in all major nuclear-related political activities in the spring of 2010. True, the Nuclear Posture Review (NPR), the Nuclear Security Summit should be regarded as evident achievements of US president. The signing of the new START agreement with Russia may also be attributed to Obama's efforts, at least partly. Well, these achievements are clear and obvious success—in political sense, especially for president Obama himself who has managed to reaffirm the rightness of choice by Nobel Peace Prize committee. Yet the picture will not be that bright if we try to look at the strategic outcome of these events.

Let's start with NPR-2010. The publishing of this document provides a good opportunity for discussing on transparency of nuclear stockpiles, importance of non-proliferation activities, on the roadmap to a world without nuclear weapons, etc. Secretary of State Hillary Clinton underlined that the declassified details about US nuclear arsenal have been released for the first time, that the NPR rules out the development of new U.S. nuclear weapons and new missions and capabilities for existing weapons and that NPR also prohibits the use of nuclear weapons against non-nuclear weapons states that are parties to the NPT and comply with its nonproliferation obligations. In reality the value of these achievements can be argued. The figures on deployed and stockpiled nuclear warheads of both USA and USSR/Russia have never been a major secret, at least for the experts, diplomats and military participating in numerous INF, SALT and START-related activities.

Dr. Gao Wanglai gives a perfect assessment of various 'side effects' of NPR in her paper "A Chinese Perspective on the Nuclear Posture Review" published on JPI PeaceNet. I will not fully agree only with her notion that "by announcing the number of its weapons, the United States enhances its security by demonstrating to the world it possesses the most superior technology in the world." The fact is that US strategic nuclear weapons have not radically changed technologically since Cold war era; the same is true for its main strategic opponent—Russia. Explanation is pretty simple: you don't need to modernize the weapons which performance is far exceeding operational demands. The parity in strategic arms between these powers still remains as it was demonstrated by signing of the new START treaty in Prague in April. And it will most likely remain until the expiration of NPR-2010 term which is declared to stay in effect till 2015-2020.

In Russia the road to the new START was not easy. The 'hawks' protested that further reductions in strategic arms would deteriorate the overall national defense capabilities while the 'realists' would prefer more deep cuts in strategic stockpiles to adjust to actual domestic situation. A number of Russian strategic systems are aging and must be retired while the industry is unable to produce the timely replacement to it. The unfortunate 'Bulava' SLBM project which is at least 5 years behind schedule is a proof of serious problems in Russian defense industry. But almost nobody argued the necessity of the treaty itself. It is remarkable: the 20+ years of military-to-military interaction in the framework of previous START mechanisms have created a unique situation of transparency, confidence building and cooperation between former strategic adversaries.

Worth noting is another definition in NPR—that spending on

US nuclear weapons complex will be increased. There is certain logic in such a decision. Nuclear warheads have its life cycle depending on plutonium contamination rate and other physical effects. Warheads must be examined, refurbished or recharged otherwise you can not rely on its performance especially with the moratorium imposed on all nuclear tests. To the other hand, additional funding provides an option for quality upgrades in existing warheads. No outsider will know for sure whether it is done to improve safety and stability of warheads or to increase its power and accuracy. The latter may easily change the fragile strategic balance in the world.

If we address the issue of non-strategic nuclear weapons it should be noted that the similar rational approach dictates its high reduction tempo. The sometimes crazy Cold war logic is over. The guaranteed self-destruction effect of massive use of tactical nuclear munitions was no secret for field commanders be it a Navy captain ordering to fire nuclear-tipped torpedo at enemy nuclear submarine or an Army colonel ready to shoot 10-inch nuclear artillery shells. Precision guided munitions can do the same job properly (if only this word is appropriate in the context) and safely today. The declared retirement of nuclear Tomahawk cruise missiles is by all means a positive step though motivated by sheer prosaic considerations again—in the new strategic environment its operational value has diminished. And if the US is seemingly ahead of Russia in retiring its non-strategic nuclear arsenal it does not mean that Washington wants to see 'a world without nuclear weapons' more than Moscow. It simply matters that US has acquired technologic superiority in conventional weapons in a number of key battlefield areas. And Russian military planners have no choice other than to continue to rely on nuclear arms in these areas. It also explains why the new Russian military doctrine (adopted in February, 2010) provides an option to use nuclear weapons first "if the very existence of Russia will be put at risk as a result of large scale 'conventional' aggression against us."

Ballistic missile defense is probably the most controversial issue today. It is well known that plans to deploy BMD elements in Eastern Europe were the main obstacle in the process of the START negotiations. The Russian reaction to these plans was a bit exaggerated, at times even hysteric. President Obama fulfilling his campaign promises has dropped this project and cleared the way to Prague-2010. But what he actually did was not a mere bargain: he has managed to remove a serious confrontational issue in US-Russian and US-European relations, saved several billions dollars to American taxpayers (it was a price of 'compensation package' to Poland and Czech Republic) and rejected a costly and operationally ineffective project. The AEGIS warships equipped with new versions of SM-3 missiles operating in Baltic, Black seas and Persian Gulf can easily outperform 10 unreliable and untested interceptors proposed for deployment in Poland. Moreover, US Navy can start ABMD patrol in European zone immediately—like they do in Korea today.

The situation around DPRK's nuclear program is highly unstable and unpredictable. It would be unfair to blame only North Koreans for their proliferation activities. Neighbor powers including USA missed at least three chances to put an end to nuclear confrontation on Korean peninsula. First, when they de facto declined to fulfill their obligations on 1994 Agreed Framework. Frozen heavy oil supplies and the view of unfinished basement instead of working LWR nuclear power plant urged Kim Jong-il to resume nuclear activities. Second, when Pyongyang had declared its withdrawal from the NPT in January, 2003 the powers pretended they did not believe in seriousness of this decision. Third, when DPRK detonated its first nuclear device in October, 2006 the reaction of Six-Party Talks' partners (except for Japan) happened to be rather strange. A clear message that world community would not tolerate NPT violators might have been enough for Pyongyang to stop its nuclear arms program.

And now we have what we have. North Korea successfully conducted a second nuclear test. Foreign experts now are busy calculating the figures of possible available warheads and means of its delivery while politicians are desperately looking for a medicine able to cure their headache—what will happen with nuclear stockpile of DPRK if Kim Jong-il's term comes to an end one day.

Unfortunately that's not all bad news. Independent observers should have noted the unusually indecisive and pacifying stance of US and its allies on tragic Cheonan incident. Sure, it's an extremely delicate issue and any mistake by politicians could lead to fatal consequences. But the 'would-be' proliferators may draw another conclusion, that it is the newly acquired nuclear weapons that stop possible aggressors from attacking North Korea. The Iran leaders may well share such an opinion. Perhaps they compare this situation with the example of its former adversary Iraq which apparently tried but failed to get nuclear arms in time to deter US-led coalition from attacking and occupying Iraqi territory.

We can see another signs or symptoms globally that convince us in necessity to strengthen the mechanisms of UN, IAEA and other international structures dealing with proliferation, nuclear safety, nuclear awareness, etc. India, Brazil, Argentina decided to build nuclear powered warships. Japan launched the extra large scale plutonium program. The youth everywhere tend to refer to nuclear arms as to something illusionary. For these reasons I guess that president Obama's nuclear-related efforts this spring should be highly appreciated. And thinking realistically I doubt that his vision of a 'world without nuclear weapons' will come true in foreseeable future. But it definitely does not mean that we can not make our world safe and secure.

---

* JPI PeaceNet No.17 published on June 29, 2010 in English

【Part 4】

Global Issue
and the Human Rights

Post-Treaty of Lisbon Changes in the EU and the Korean Response

KO Sangtu

Yonsei University

❚ EU in the Changing International Order

The recent global economic crisis, continuing progress with the European integration, and the rise of Newly Industrialized Countries has led to a shift in international order. International order has transformed from the bipolar system in the Cold War era and uni-polar system in the Post Cold War era, and it is expected to undergo yet another turn to the multi-polar system. There are many scenarios about the future landscape of the international society; G2 theory with an emphasis on the leadership of China and the US, BRICs Emergence theory with an emphasis on geographic territory and population dominance, and the Global

Cooperation theory with an emphasis on the role of the G20 are just a few of them. Signing of the Treaty of Lisbon for the EU presents us with another very plausible alternative system of G3. The EU has put a great weight on soft power in fields such as environment, human rights, and welfare, and it is now seeking to enhance its hard power through trade, financial aids and peacekeeping operations.

▌Key Elements of the Lisbon System

The Treaty of Lisbon has enhanced the European Union (EU)'s internal authority. Until very recently, the EU was merely a political identity, and it was legally represented by the former European Community (EC). In other words, European countries did not take legal measures to put a stamp on the integration even though they reached a political consensus to push forward with it. However, the Treaty of Lisbon has made the EU an actual legal entity, rather than a political identity, and all of the EU's authorities have become legally binding.

EU's scope of power has been greatly expanded by the Treaty of Lisbon. It will now be responsible for all matters like political affairs, environment, and security, as well as economic affairs on which the EU's activities have mostly been focused. In the past, there were distinctions between the EU's authority, EU and members' shared authority, and members' authority. But the treaty has made affairs in all areas subject to the EU's power. Furthermore, the policy decision-making process has become simplified. The majority rule is now applied to all issues save military and taxation affairs.

EU's external authority has also been enhanced. The offices of so called EU President (2.5-year term) and High Representative of Foreign and Security Affairs (5-year term) have newly opened inside the European Council, and the High Representative is to launch and directly lead the EEAS. The EU currently has 5,000 diplomats dispatched to 130 overseas offices, and 1/3 of them are expected to be replaced in the near future. For this end, it plans to solicit assistance from each member with an introduction of 1,200~1,300 diplomacy professionals to its HR pool. They will be employed at the EU for 4 years and return to their home country under the rotation employment system. This change institutionalizes the direct participation of all members in the EU's international affairs.

▌ EU-Korea Relationship after Treaty of Lisbon

The Treaty of Lisbon is expected to drastically change the EU-

Korea trade and investment environment. First and foremost, simplification of the legislation process at the EU will lead to a considerable increase in the number of decisions related to environment, safety, and technology regulations. Similarly, the standardization and unification of various codes and systems in Europe are likely to accelerate.

Second, the environment for the EU-Korea FTA ratification has changed. The consent from the European Parliament is now necessary, and there is a possibility that European businesses against the FTA ratification would exert their influence over the political leaders. The Automobile Manufacturers' Associations in Germany and Italy are already voicing their criticism that the EU has handed over an advantage in the manufacturing sector for gains in the finance and intellectual property sectors. Some say that the EU Trade Commissioner Ashton who was in charge of the FTA negotiation with Korea was from the UK, and that she neglected the interests of manufacturing industries.

The use of Euro as the currency for international bank settlement among European countries is expected to increase. EU's public finance and financial affairs authorities have greatly increased, and it now has a strong influence over the countries that are yet to introduce the Euro. It is also highly likely that the Euro Zone will expand. Many non-Euro Zone countries recorded high economic growth rates prior to the global financial crisis. However, most, if not all, of them experienced a severe currency instability in the face of a financial crisis, and they are positively considering joining the Euro Zone. The expansion of the Euro Zone will essentially speed up the process of Euro becoming the key currency. Accordingly, Korea will need to consider a change in the foreign currency reserve policy in a timely manner.

The EU and Korea amended the existing Framework Agreement for Cooperation to promise all-encompassing cooperation in the non economic areas, and the bilateral relationship has been upgraded to a strategic partnership. The EU is rather stringent in bestowing the strategic partnership "honor" upon non-European countries; and Korea has become the EU's 8th strategic partner. This marks the beginning of the Pan West Diplomacy Era for Korea, with the U.S. as an ally and the EU as a strategic partner.

The EU wants to share and jointly take measures to protect the general values of democracy, human rights, and environment with Korea. In short, it is trying to form a value community with Korea. Hence, Korea needs to establish a cooperative relationship that meets the EU's expectation by increasing its efforts and investments in the non-proliferation of weapons of mass destruction and joint response against terrorism in the foreign affairs and security areas, prevention of organized crimes and money laundering in the internal and legal affairs areas, and the reduction of the greenhouse gas emission and promotion of sustainable development in the environment area.

In this regard, the EU and Korea's strategic objectives are China and North Korea. The EU's foreign policy places a great emphasis on the rule of law. Unlike sovereign states that have national interest as the objective of their foreign policy, the EU, as a supranational organization, puts more weight on the observation of universal norm. There are many exchange activities between China and the EU, but the human rights problem in China is making the qualitative improvement of the cooperation difficult, not to mention hindering the bilateral FTA negotiation between them.

In addition, Korea plays an important role in the EU's China policy. The EU believes that Korea's cooperation can influence China. Should Korea, along with Japan, present China with an advanced development that incorporates environmental, free trade, and human rights issues, China is likely to change accordingly. The rule of law is also of importance in the EU's North Korea policy. The EU is taking a proactive stand on North Korea's democracy, human rights, and nuclear issues. It was the first to openly criticize North Korea's nuclear test, and it has been leading numerous discussions on the Resolutions on Sanctions against

North Korea at the UN Human Rights Council. Therefore, we need to establish a cooperation system to affect North Korea by tying in the human rights protection and humanitarian support of which the EU has the greatest interest.

---

* JPI PeaceNet No.4 published on March 2, 2010 in Korean

U.S. and China Human Rights Dialogues and Prospect of the Human Rights Issue in East Asia

YI Seong-Woo
Jeju Peace Institute

▌The Importance of Human Rights Dialogues between the U.S. and China

The US-China Human Rights Dialogue was held in a closed-door session in Washington DC on May 13 and 14, 2010. In international relations, the human rights issue has been put behind national security and economy in terms of priority. However, it is also true that China, which seeks to refresh its image as a world power, should consider human rights as a necessary condition for the development of its relations with other countries. This paper attempts to check the significance of the human rights issue in international relations on the occasion of the dialogue between the two world powers and the interactions between human rights policies and international politics in East Asia.

Such a dialogue between the two countries was also held in March 2004, but China withdrew from it in response to the U.S. submittal of a resolution blaming the human rights situation in China in the annual meeting of the UN Human Rights Commission. In May 2008, the Chinese government agreed to the resumption of the dialogue in an effort to interrupt the movement of western human rights organizations to stage protest demonstrations or boycott the Beijing Olympics slated for August of the same year concerning imprisonment of anti-regime activists in China. The Chinese government has taken a proactive attitude to block movements in the international community about the human rights issue involving it. In February 2008, Chinese Foreign Minister Yang Jiechi agreed to a meeting with the U.S. State Secretary Condoleezza Rice in China, saying that his country was ready to exchange opinions on his country's human rights situation with other countries on the condition of mutual respect and equality and no interference in internal affairs. This bilateral meeting is the one held after a two year interval after the one held in May 2008. It was originally scheduled for February this year, but was postponed with China protesting the U.S. sale of weapons to Taiwan and U.S. President Barack Obama's acceptance of a meeting with Tibetan religious leader Dalai Lama.

Major Agenda Items at the 2010 U.S.-China Human Rights Dialogue

The 2010 U.S.-China Human Rights Dialogue was attended by officials representing the State Department, the Justice Department, the Department of Homeland Security, the Labor Department, the Commerce Department, the IRS, and the USTR on the U.S. side and the foreign minister Chenhsu, officials representing the Judicial Branch of the government, the Ministry of Public Security, the Ministry of Religious Affairs, the Supreme People's Court on the Chinese side. They discussed matters, such as freedom of religion, workers' rights, freedom of expression, rules of law, racial discrimination, multipartite collaboration, along with individual cases in the stated areas. In such a respect, the U.S.-China Human Rights Dialogue made a comprehensive approach, but the result was not quite satisfactory.

In a press briefing, Michael Posner, Assistant Secretary of State for Democracy, Human Rights and Labor, said that the two countries exchanged comprehensive ideas about the human rights issues of the two countries in the bilateral dialogue and the U.S. regards it as a significant step forward. Such a comment shows that the two sides view the meeting itself as significant rather than trying to obtain noticeable agreements or substantial improvements in the human rights situation in China. The U.S.

raised the following concerning the human rights issue in China: (1) Withdrawal of Google from China in connection with Internet-related freedom and censorship, (2) the issue concerning Tibet and Xinjiang Weiwuer in connection with freedom of religion and the Dalai Lama, (3) the issue concerning Falun Gong in connection with the freedom of expression, and (4) the safety of Chinese-made food imported into the U.S.

The U.S. also took issue with individual cases of human rights violations in China. Concerning Gao Zhisheng, an imprisoned human rights lawyer and member of Falun Gong, the U.S. took issue with the rights of criminal suspects and the legal procedure. However, it is not known whether there was a discussion on the human rights activist Liu Xiaobo. The U.S. appears to avoid making a direct comment on sensitive issues, such as the current location of the anti-regime/human rights activists, including Gao Zhisheng, and the status of conscientious prisoners.

Concerning the North Korean, Cambodian and Burmese escapees staying in China, the U.S. said that it was necessary to continue to take protective measures for them. Although the human rights issue concerning the North Korean escapees was dealt with at the meeting, details such as the need to stop sending them back forcefully to North Korea and recognize their status as refugees were not.

As an offensive measure against the U.S., China took issue with the U.S. government's (potential) radical discrimination against minorities concerning the Immigration Law of the State of Arizona in the U.S.

∎ The Significance of the 2010 U.S.-China Human Rights Dialogue

The U.S. government makes a generally affirmative appraisal about the 2010 U.S.-China Human Rights Dialogue. As for the areas where the most development was made through the meeting, the U.S. side pointed to improvements made in China's understanding of the need for the independence of the Judicial Branch of the government, the rules of law, and attorneys appointed by the courts for criminal defendants not able to afford one. However, it remains doubtable how much China will reflect such a demand in its justice system realistically. In connection with the past case in which the dialogue was stopped, it might have been a positive development of the meeting that the U.S. made it clear that it would not refer the human rights situation in China to the UN Human Rights Commission. It appears that China expressed some voluntariness in the need for improvement of its human rights situation during the dialogue. Concerning the dialogue to be held in 2011, China consented to it, although the date has not been fixed, and agreed to the need for a periodical meeting like this.

The civic human rights organizations make a generally negative appraisal of the bilateral human rights dialogue. They pointed to the closed sessions, which made the contents of the dialogue not transparent. However, the U.S. government stressed that it thought that the two countries could work together to bridge the differences through discussion.

Concerning the background of the 2010 US-China Human Rights Dialogue, the U.S. government explains that it was held separately from the U.S.-China Strategic and Economic Dialogue held in Beijing toward the end of May 2010. The U.S.-China Strategic and Economic Dialogue is held for discussion about short and long-term strategic and economic challenges and opportunities faced by the two countries bilaterally, regionally and worldwide. Thus, the two countries say that it has nothing to do with the human rights issue, but the reality is not like that. As for China, it cannot avoid the human rights dialogue with the U.S. and the U.S. finds it difficult to pressurize China hard in connection with its human rights situation considering its status as a partner of the strategic and economic dialogue. International human rights watchers ask the U.S. for a more proactive stance, saying that it is not a proper measure to separate the two dialogues. The U.S. human rights organizations have pointedly denounced the U.S. government, saying that it has turned a blind eye on the human rights situation in China to win the country's support in issues concerning North Korea, Iran and climatic changes.

In international relations, the human rights issue has made considerable progress over the past 30 years. In the late 1970s, when U.S. President Jimmy Carter adopted the human rights diplomacy, many countries regarded a country's mention of another country's human rights situation as interference in the internal affairs of a sovereign state. The change in the international order in the post-cold war period and the changes in the value upholding democracy and peace brought about a new concept of human security. Under such circumstances, human rights became an absolute criterion as a universal human value and sovereignty of a state became a matter of relative importance. However, despite such a change in value, countries like China show a strong resistance against another country's mention of its human rights situation, blaming it as a serious interference in another country's internal affairs. Thus, it requires a cautious approach.

South Korea may find it necessary to set its human rights policy concerning the human rights situation in neighboring countries based on the following U.S. strategy on the human rights situation in China in connection with the U.S.-China Strategic and Economic Dialogue. (1) It is necessary to remind China that the U.S. may always raise the human rights issue in China unless the situation improves noticeably and that the issue is a necessary condition to the development of the bilateral relations. (2) The U.S. should continue to mention the human rights situation in China, adjusting the scope and intensity in a way that China cannot reject the relevant discussion. The U.S. should approach the subject strategically, wisely using dialogues and projects of mutual collaboration. The U.S. may continue to discuss the human rights issue and win China's collaboration when it uses a method of raising human rights-related principles, such as the rules of law or the freedom of expression rather than pointing directly to the individual human rights activists, such as the Dalai Lama, Gao Zhisheng or Liu Xiaobo. (3) Concerning the human rights situation in China, the U.S. needs to take a dual approach. First, the U.S. should stop thinking that raising the human rights issue concerning China is a policy tool for the attainment of its diplomatic objective. The U.S. needs to take a cautious strategic approach to the matters, such as workers' human rights, trade barriers, Internet-related business activities, the safety of Chinese-made food, etc., are associated with the U.S. economic interest in the Chinese market. (4) In connection with the strategic needs stated in the foregoing, the U.S. needs to set up objectives and principles concerning the human rights situation in China and deliver it to China in clear terms based on the understanding that presentation of clear objectives concerning the human rights issues will help China improve the relevant situation through the bilateral dialogues.

Progress in the U.S.-China human rights dialogue can serve as an important leverage on other Asian countries that have paid little attention to their human rights situation. They may watch the bilateral dialogue with hopeful expectations as it may become the starting point for an effort to overcome heterogeneous values of countries in the region that will comprise an East Asian Community. The fostering of the atmosphere conducive to the improvement of the human rights situation through the U.S.-China human rights dialogue will help South Korea secure relevant policy means concerning the human rights issue relating to North Korea and China.

---

* JPI PeaceNet No.15 published on June 15, 2010 in Korean

The Euro Zone's Economic Crisis and the Future of Monetary Collaboration between East Asian Countries

CHAI Hee Yul
Kyonggi University

I The Euro Zone's Economic Crisis

The international financial market seemed to be recovering from the shock of the global financial crisis that started in 2008 and regaining stability in early 2010, although it underwent further violent turbulence due to the financial difficulty of certain countries in Southern Europe, notably Greece and Portugal. The violent turbulence of the market, despite the relatively small size of the economy of these problematic countries, was due to the strong doubts raised about the sustainability of the euro and the euro zone as indicated by the sharp drop in the value of the euro against other major currencies, in addition to the fairly large amount of loans made to these countries by the financial institutions of leading European countries.

Thus, euro-zone leaders responded to the situation positively, announcing a bailout plan for Greece and their willingness to mobilize all available means to secure the stability of the euro zone. It goes without saying that their joint countermeasures were not taken without some dissent. France and Italy insisted that the support for Greece should be provided by the euro zone alone, while Germany, Sweden and Finland said that the IMF should take part in the support plan. Ultimately, Germany's position was adopted, as the final decision asked for the euro zone's assumption of two-thirds of the bailout money, with the remainder left to the responsibility of the IMF.

It appears that the euro-zone economy has recently regained some stability and the euro has rebounded as a result of such support from the member countries. However, the sovereign risk of some countries still remains high, and it is thought that the crisis, which currently remains below the surface, may reemerge at any time. Although economic recovery is predicted in the leading euro-zone countries, such as Germany and France, the situation in countries in Southern Europe, such as Greece, Spain and Portugal, remains uncertain and it is feared that these problematic countries may remain vulnerable to economic crisis on a prolonged basis.

Causes of the Euro Zone's Economic Crisis

The causes of the euro zone's economic crisis have been attributed to the problems concerning the process of forming a single currency sphere, as well as some countries' reckless financial operations and excessive welfare expenditure. In the 60-year-long process of deepening and expanding the goal of integration of the European economy, economic logic and political considerations have served as a crucial locomotive. The launch of the European Coal and Steel Community (ECSC) in 1951 was a result of the expectation that a solidary European body would work importantly for the maintenance of peace in the region. The reinforcement of political solidarity served as an important motive in the launch of the European Economic Community (EEC) and the European Monetary System (EMS) in the ensuing period, as well as in the process of European integration and spillover expansion, with a shift from the focus on Northern and Southern European countries to the inclusion of Central and Eastern European countries. The same could be said of the launch of the euro.

The formation of a single currency sphere has merits, such as the invigoration of trade and human exchanges within the sphere, and the promotion of the currency's international use, but it also entails a problem: the lack of a monetary policy or an exchange rate-related policy makes it very difficult for individual countries to remedy their state of recession or an economic imbalance such as a deficit in their current account balance. To minimize such problems, a single currency should be adopted by countries that have a similar business cycle and industrial competitiveness, and healthy macroeconomic fundamentals. With this taken into account, European countries signed the Maastricht Treaty, which stipulated that only those countries which met the considerably strict conditions could join the euro zone. However, most of the countries that wished to join the euro zone were allowed to join the European Economic and Monetary Union (EMU) in 1999, as they reached the consensus that political solidarity was more important, and only a few countries were able to meet the strict conditions. As for Greece, which fell far short of the criteria for fiscal deficit and financial liabilities, it joined the euro zone in 2001 as a result of manipulation of the relevant statistics and political considerations.

The inherent limitation concerning the launch of the euro zone lies in the fact that the participation in monetary integration of member states that were unqualified to do so was permitted out of purely political considerations. Thus, the problem of regional deficit in the current account balance worsened, particularly on the part of those Southern European countries that remained weak in terms of industrial competitiveness. During globally good times, even these countries recorded high growth and their structural problems remained below the surface. However, with the entire world hit by the financial crisis in 2008, their problems came to the surface, resulting in the worsening of their fiscal balance and an increase in their foreign debt.

▌ Lessons to Be Learned from Europe Concerning Monetary Collaboration between East Asian Countries

At present, no currency holds hegemony in East Asia and the U.S. dollar has absolute dominance in all functions (i.e. denomination, payment and store of value) of an international currency. However, it is predicted that the Chinese yuan may emerge as a regional key currency in 20 to 30 years, given the ongoing enhancement of the status of the Chinese economy on almost a daily basis. The fact that the Chinese economy lacks transparency or openness and that its capital market still remains at the inceptive stage will work as inhibitors of such a prospect. Nonetheless, if that country opens its capital market and establishes a transparent economic policy system, its currency may emerge as a key currency in the region on the back of the rapid growth of its economy and the heavy dependence of regional trades on China. The Chinese yuan's emergence as a hegemonic currency in the region cannot be left unattended as a matter for the distant future, when the country is taking a series of steps aimed at the internationalization of its currency.

With the Chinese yuan emerging as a key currency in the region, the neighboring countries' dependence on it will deepen further still, even in monetary and financial sectors. That is not desirable politically for the neighboring countries. The neighboring countries are also likely to lose their monetary sovereignty. In addition, they will be affected to a greater extent in the event of unease in the Chinese economy. Thus, it is desirable to create a third single currency through monetary collaboration between the countries in the region. As a country that is under U.S. pressure for the appreciation of its currency, China is not necessarily negative about the need for monetary collaboration in the region: Hence the possibility of persuading China towards the said goal.

The problem lies in determining which countries will be in the same boat of monetary collaboration. If the entire ASEAN+3 countries are allowed to join out of solely political considerations, as in the case of Europe, the block thus formed will only remain weak. It will be desirable to push ahead with the goal of monetary collaboration in East Asia, with the priority placed on such factors as whether they are at a similar stage of economic development and whether they operate a transparent policy and statistical system. However, too much stress on economic factors will limit the candidate countries to only a few, given that the economic circumstances and exchange rates in the countries in the region move very asymmetrically with each other and their respective rates of industrial competitiveness vary considerably. Moreover, as the chief aim of the monetary collaboration would be to check the emergence of the Chinese yuan as a hegemonic currency, the formation of a block among a limited number of countries, particularly with China excluded, would not serve the intended purpose. Thus, monetary collaboration between countries in East Asia needs to be promoted by maintaining a proper balance between political and economic considerations.

Finally, the current economic crisis experienced by Europe does not appear to reveal only negative aspects of monetary integration. Greece and Portugal are going through a financial crisis, but not a foreign currency liquidity crisis. The reason for this is that their local currency is now the euro, i.e. an international currency. In contrast, South Korea had to face the foreign currency liquidity difficulty, despite its healthy basic macroeconomic fundamentals in 1997. If a single currency is adopted and it secures its position as an international currency in East Asia, a country like South Korea, which operates a healthy economy and maintains solid industrial competitiveness, will be able to establish a more stable posture against a possible crisis.

---

* JPI PeaceNet No.22 published on September 3, 2010 in Korean

International Cooperation on Natural Disasters

HA Kyoo-Man
Inje Institute of Advanced Studies

As experienced by the recent earthquake disaster in Haiti and the flood ravages in Pakistan, a large-scale natural disaster affects a large area and thus requires international cooperation. A typhoon strike, for example, causes damages to several countries. Thus, it is necessary to maintain a system of international cooperation at all times.

Sometimes, natural disaster management is carried out by the private sector, but the overall responsibility is taken by state institutions, considering its nature related to public welfare. In Korea, the National Emergency Management Agency (NEMA), a subsidiary institution of the Ministry Of Public Administration and

Security (MOPAS), is in charge of the disaster-related business. At the time of its launch in June 2004, the NEMA remained at an inception stage concerning international cooperation. Now, six year later, the NEMA is carrying out natural disaster-related international exchanges briskly in cooperation with the Ministry Of Foreign Affairs and Trade (MOFAT). It dispatched a rescue team to the Sichuan Province, China when it was hit by an earthquake in May 2008. It hosted the 4th Asian Ministerial Conference on Disaster Risk Reduction in October 2010. Recently, the amount of donations made by the South Korean government to the international community concerning natural disasters has increased considerably, although some watchers say that the amount should be raised in consideration of the economic strength of the country. Despite such brisk activities and efforts, the South Korean government, particularly the NEMA, leaves many things to be desired concerning natural disasters and international cooperation. This paper intends to point out five macroscopic problems and proposes solutions to them as follows:

First, the country carries out its natural disaster-related cooperation mostly with Asian countries, such as China, Japan, Mongolia, and Southeast Asian countries. It dispatched a rescue team to the site of the earthquake in China and made joint efforts to reduce the occurrence of yellow dust in Mongolia. It also maintains relations of cooperation with neighboring countries not directly affected by natural disasters through joint seminars or conferences or disaster manager training sessions.

Those from neighboring countries who took part in programs of international cooperation offered by the country usually expressed satisfaction with such programs. However, the country tends to pay little attention to cooperation with faraway countries. When Haiti and Chile were hit by severe earthquakes in January and February 2010, it was pointed out that the level of cooperation, including donation amount, provided by South Korea was not generous enough. Unlike South Korea, China dispatched a large-scale aid team, although it was difficult to land planes at airports in Haiti. Haiti and U.S. mass media spoke highly of what China did to help a country in need. In such a respect, the country needs to consider positive ripple effects brought by the provision of disaster-related aid to faraway countries from a long-term perspective.

Second, in South Korea, government institutions play a leading role in the provision of natural disasters-related aid, including that provided by the NEMA. Sometimes, civilians participate in such aid with financial support provided by their organizations. Civilians (both organizations and individuals) have limitations in their capacity of carrying out such aid. International cooperation for such aid requires a lot of expenses, making it difficult for small-sized civilian organizations to make an attempt to help. However, there are many volunteer organizations and individuals willing to help those in faraway foreign countries out of humanitarianism. The South Korean government should consider such a fact in carrying out disaster-related international aid programs. The Korean Red Cross and leading NGOs of the country are huge-sized organizations and they can go a long way in cooperation with the government in carrying out such programs.

Third, the country needs to carry out such aid programs, fully utilizing retired, but internationally influential people, including former Presidents or Prime Ministers, particularly in the case of international programs, as it can double the effect, as the U.S. does in cases of disasters that requires international cooperation.

Fourth, the NEMA has made virtually no inter-border disaster-related cooperation with North Korea. At present, the Ministry of Unification controls matters concerning cooperation with North Korea. The NEMA needs to carry out relevant research in preparation for future needs, utilizing the existing organizations and personnel.

Fifth, the country needs to publicize its activities in natural disaster-related international cooperation, utilizing foreign mass media in connection with the need to reinforce the country's reputation worldwide, while making such activities with a focus on the reduction of loss of human lives and property. According to foreign press reports, the rescue team dispatched by the Chinese government held up its national flag high and shouted the slogan upon arrival in Haiti. U.S. mass media covering the earthquake in Haiti sent out the news of their government's rescue effort at their evening news. In July 2010, when Pakistan suffered from a large-scale flood, the U.S. media did similarly concerning their government's rehabilitation aid efforts. The South Korean government needs to have its efforts made in foreign countries known throughout the world through cooperation between the NEMA and MOFAT and coordination with foreign mass media.

* JPI PeaceNet No.23 published on September 6, 2010 in Korean

Emergence of G30 and the Need for a New World Financial Order

LEE Sang-hwan
Hankuk University of Foreign Studies

In two months time, the G20 Summit will be held in Seoul, heralding the start of a new world financial and economic order in the wake of the global financial crisis. The outline of the policy direction concerning sustainable and balanced growth, which is the priority item on the agenda of the G20 Summit, is expected to be presented at the forthcoming event in Seoul. At the Toronto Summit held last June, the leaders of the G20 countries agreed to discuss new international capital and cash liquidity criteria designed to reinforce bank soundness regulation and new ways of innovating international financial organizations, including the International Monetary Fund (IMF), at the Seoul Summit.

The G20, which was launched as an alternative to the G7 in connection with the need to overcome the global financial crisis, is a de facto supreme council dealing with global economic issues. The launch of the G7 was a result of the first oil shock in the early 1970s and the ensuing instability of the world economy. At that time, a more fundamental cause of such instability was the collapse of the Bretton Woods system and the adoption of a system of fluctuating exchange rates.

From the time of its launch, the G20 was closely connected with financial crisis. The foreign exchange/financial crisis that hit various countries in East Asia in 1997 drove not only Asian countries, including South Korea, but the world economy into confusion. Leading industrialized countries saw that the financial crises in newly emerging countries could cause financial instability in themselves as a result of globalization. Thus, they started looking for ways of cooperation with newly emerging countries to prevent the recurrence of such a disaster. The G20 system has gradually revealed itself, following the first meeting of the financial ministers and central bank presidents of the G20 countries in Berlin in December 1999.

The G20 is a club composed of the twenty leading economies of the world, i.e. the G7 (the U.S., the U.K., France, Germany, Italy, Japan and Canada), the EU, the BRICs (Brazil, Russia, India and

China), and eight emerging economies (South Korea, Indonesia, Argentina, Mexico, Turkey, Australia, South Africa, and Saudi Arabia). Today, the G20 accounts for roughly 85% of the world's GDP and two-third's of the world's population, displaying its influence and representativeness. It is particularly significant that, with the launch of the G20 Summit, emerging countries have secured an active position in the search for a new world financial order.

It can be said that the shift to the G20 system was a natural course of action following the global economic crisis and the change in the distribution of economic power between countries. As it has sufficient economic representativeness, the G20 will only be able to consolidate its position as an established system if it can secure effectiveness. The problem is that it is not easy to find the means by which the member countries, which hold diverse positions from the perspective of national interest, can reach a consensus and put it into action.

Some scholars say that the share of emerging countries in the world economy will expand to about 70% in ten years. While the G20 has emerged to replace the G7, there are people voicing the need for the launch of a G30, which would include some of the poor countries of Africa. They say that global economic and financial issues cannot now be settled by either the leading industrialized countries or by a small group of countries, including newly industrialized countries, and that they can only be settled by the proposed G30. The prevailing situation in the 1970s required collaboration between the G7 countries. The G20 was launched according to the dictates of the situation in the 1990s. And what is happening today leads experts to predict the emergence of a G30.

The G20 is composed of five groups of regional leading countries (i.e. industrialized and emerging countries), namely, Group 1 (the U.S., Canada, Saudi Arabia and Australia), Group 2 (Russia, India, Turkey and South Africa), Group 3 (Brazil, Argentina and Mexico), Group 4 (the U.K., France, Germany and Italy) and Group 5 (South Korea, Japan, China and Indonesia). In contrast, the G30 will be a body that represents the whole world, including late-starting industrial countries and poor countries in Africa, Asia and Latin America. It may be said to be a transitional course in the move toward the status of genuine global governance. The central of the world economy has laid in major industrialized countries amid the emphasis on effectiveness. However, the discussion about the launch of a G30 is meaningful in that the global consensus in the true meaning of the word should secure its representativeness based on negotiations and mutual agreements rather than on strength.

How, then, should we view the emergence of the proposed G30? In discussions about the significance of the G20, some watchers express their view that the Anglo-American style market-oriented system will decline and be replaced by the influence of governments in the future world financial/economic order, and thus that it will be difficult to create a wide-ranging bubble economy in various regions of the world as in the past. They insist that priority should be placed on the establishment of a system that can control market-related risks rather than on deregulation. Their policy position is that the positive functions of deregulation should be maximized, but market-related risks caused by deregulation should be thoroughly controlled.

In early 2009, the Group of Thirty (G-30), formed in 1978 and composed a body of economists and policy makers from many countries around the world, released the Report on How to Improve the Financial System. The report contains ideas about how to expand governmental regulations on banks and their investment business in an epoch-making way. It points to the need to limit the size of banks and regulate their managers' remunerations, hedge funds and the concentration of deposits on a small number of banks. Their point is that it is necessary not to allow the failure of each institution to have structural importance by reducing its size, and that the same logic should apply to all financial institutions similar to banks and their products.

Concerning the possibility of preventing a global financial crisis through financial innovation, George Soros said: "Markets are not only imperfect but bubbles are likely to occur as they do not always succeed in balancing themselves. Financial authorities should check the status of the market and emit a warning sound at an opportune time." What he says is that it is not easy to regulate the financial market uniformly and that we cannot be confident about the effects of regulations. As such, we should focus on innovations by reinforcing the supervisory system that copes well with the structural characteristics of the financial market rather than by expanding uniform regulations. In this regard, collaboration between countries appears to be all the more important, and we expect a more positive role of the G30, which will take a one step forward from the G20.

In 2008, the G20 Summit was launched as a new world economic council due to a perceived need for close policy collaboration between industrialized countries and emerging countries amid the effort to settle the global financial crisis that started in the U.S.. What enabled emerging countries to take part in the efforts to overcome the financial crisis shoulder to shoulder with industrialized countries was the enhanced status of such countries as South Korea, China and India. Now, they are discussing the launch of a G30 that would include even some poor countries, pointing to the forthcoming launch of genuine global governance.

* JPI PeaceNet No.24 published on September 14, 2010 in Korean

US Human Rights Policy toward China

James MEERNIK
University of North Texas

The United States government has labored persistently and strenuously to improve China's human rights practices for many years. Despite such efforts by Democrats and Republicans, Presidents and the U.S. Congress, there have been relatively few victories achieved as measured against the effort exerted. To be sure, without such pressure human rights practices may have worsened in some cases and many prominent, Chinese human rights activists might not have been released. Yet, since the thawing of relations between the U.S. and China in the 1970's, and especially after the Tiananmen Square incident in 1989, Chinese human rights conditions have changed predominantly in response to Chinese interests rather than US attempts to shame or coerce improvements. The chart below, using the well-known Cingrinelli-Richards scale of human rights protection and measured on a 0-8 scale, shows the ebb and flow of human rights over time in China. Despite continual pressure on China regarding political prisoners, religious freedom, Tibetan rights, family planning and attempts to link changes in such policies to Most Favored Nation Status, WTO membership, and a host of other issues, Chinese human rights protections still rank among the lowest in the world. I argue here that however one might conceptualize or measure human rights in China, the United States will likely not exact significant, systemic human rights changes in China with its current approach.

First, and perhaps foremost, to exert influence over another nation on issues that have profound consequences for sovereignty requires considerable power and leverage. The US has significant influence in some policy areas because of its military hegemony, close ties with key neighboring states, its intellectual capital and other tools. But because the United States is so dependent upon

Chinese Human Rights, 1981-2008

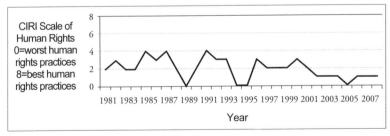

China to finance its ever-growing debt burden, China holds the ultimate trump card in their relationships. China is the largest holder of US debt (approximately 846 billion dollars in July 2010) (http://www.ustreas.gov/tic/mfh.txt). The US also imports very heavily from China and has used its cheaply-priced goods to keep the U.S. cost of living quite low. Given such dependency, the debtor nation is hardly in a position to bargain, especially on a matter vital to Chinese interests. The Chinese understand this power disparity and can, with a well-timed comment regarding their willingness to purchase more US debt, influence the U.S. economy. The United States economic dependence on China diminishes the degree of leverage the U.S. can exert on China, while the Chinese dependence upon American willingness to buy its products does not accord a similar degree of U.S. influence over China.

The U.S. has also politicized the cause of human rights by linking it to various and sundry other policy initiatives vis a vis China (most especially economic issues), by condoning violations of human rights by other governments when US national interests are at stake, and by countenancing its own violations of human rights in the war on terror. Such actions, while understandable and predictable from a realpolitik perspective, become the counter-arguments used by others to point out the flaws and hypocrisy in U.S. admonitions on human rights. If human rights are excusable against terrorists then labeling regime opponents as terrorists can deflect criticism. If the U.S. is lukewarm in its condemnation of human rights abuses perpetrated by friendly governments in Africa or Asia, the Chinese can then argue the promotion of such goals is meant to serve a national interest rather than a global value. All such debates ultimately serve to confuse and conflate human rights with politics, which tarnishes the reputation of the ideal and undermines the arguments of states like the U.S. that seek to advance this cause. Politicization of human rights undermines the cause and provides the Chinese ample ammunition to question U.S. sincerity and deflect US attempts to change its practices.

Promotion of human rights in China is also extremely difficult because of China's deep and enduring concern for its sovereignty rights. Hence, as a result of strong sovereignty norms we see China's predicable and marked antipathy toward Western "naming and shaming" campaigns that seek to bring pressure on governments to reform their policies. U.S. efforts to push Chinese leaders to open up their political processes and take steps to insure personal integrity rights will generally run afoul of leaders with long memories of past periods of upheaval and concern for their own political survival. As well, with such an immense bureaucracy with vested interest in the maintenance of the Chinese political system, the US is no more apt to gain traction against such powerful actors than it is to move its own massive bureaucracy to enact fundamental reform.

Thus, we must ask whether U.S. foreign policy ever has any prospect at any level to influence human rights conditions in China. Attempts at encouraging the Chinese to modify their political system may have some beneficial impact at the systemic level, if only as a constant reminder of the importance of this cause to the U.S. and its fellow Western democracies. I argue, however, that those efforts that focus on particular individuals and certain groups whose agenda does not pose a significant challenge to communist party rule are the areas in which the United States is most likely to be successful. Efforts on behalf of individuals and groups of individuals arrested en masse (e.g., lawyers whose clients are themselves human rights activists) are likely to be most effective. Individuals per se typically do not pose a substantial threat to regime stability, regardless of the rhetoric used by the Chinese government to characterize their activities. Thus, concessions here are not likely to be perceived as systemically destabilizing. Furthermore, such efforts can be made in meetings and discussions with Chinese leaders rather than through press releases or congressional reports in which compliance would likely be viewed as capitulation. Human rights issues involving entire groups of people such as Tibetans or Uighurs are also more likely to result in improvements through encouragement of negotiation rather than condemnation.

Ultimately, China is most likely to open its political system and improve human rights because of economics and not politics. The demands of the global economy and the age of information will encourage greater transparency, rule of law, and human freedom. Those states that embrace these virtues are best positioned to prosper in this economy. Those states that do not permit such practices or only weakly so will reach a growth limit beyond which further prosperity depends on greater freedoms. Where wealth ultimately depends on the ability to generate the ideas and information necessary to develop the most desirable goods and services, those states that allow for the freest exchange and development of ideas will be at a competitive advantage. China will be prodded to progressively open its political system and expand political rights to allow for such a free exchange of ideas, much as it has progressively opened its system to allow for the free exchange of goods and labor. The global convergence toward such best practices in political and human rights, while allowing for local variations as necessary, will eventually change China. But it will be the invisible hand of the market place rather than the mailed fist of the superpower that finally accomplishes this transformation.

Finally, educational exchanges are an extremely important venue for advancing the cause of human rights. Programs led by U.S. universities in China or that bring Chinese students to the United

States to study key subjects such as political science, economics, philosophy, sociology, history and especially law can greatly expand the size of the intellectual community supporting human rights. As well, more foreign students are coming to China to study and more Chinese students are going abroad. This global flow of people and ideas will also advance efforts to bring greater concern for human freedom and rights into the Chinese political system. The decades ahead will bring many changes in the power and influence of the United States and China that have the potential to create political conflict and instability. But there are grounds for hope that as China begins to take seriously the cause of human rights, these inevitable disputes can be managed at the negotiating table.

---

* JPI PeaceNet No.30 published on October 26, 2010 in English

Human Rights and Sovereignty in the Era of Global Governance

SOH Changrok
Korea University

There is a controversy over the designation of Liu Xiaobo, an anti-regime activist in China, as the Nobel Peace Prize winner for 2010. He is an intellectual who has been engaged in a non-violence struggle for years asking for democracy and improvement of the human rights situation in China. He is also known as the symbol of the Tiananmen Incident of 1976. The Chinese government imprisoned him on a charge of instigating anti-regime activities. At present, he is in prison.

U.S. President Barack Obama welcomed the news of Liu's designation as the Nobel Peace Prize winner as the leaders of Western countries did. Concerning Liu's efforts for improvement of the human rights situation in China, President Obama said, "He is a figure who has spoken for the advancement of universal values persuasively and courageously" and urged for his immediate release to the Chinese government. In response, the Chinese Foreign Ministry criticized Obama's remarks as an act encouraging a crime. It added that the designation of Liu Xiaobo as the Nobel Peace Prize winner itself is an act of ignoring the justice system of China and the event would not have any impact on the country's regime. It also said that the Chinese government would regard criticisms made by Western countries as interference in internal matters. Outraged, the Chinese government cancelled a scheduled fishery minister meeting with Norway, summoned its ambassador to Norway, and stopped all cultural exchanges with that country.

On October 21, U.S. Attorney General Eric Holder said that there was a fundamental disagreement between his country and China, speaking about Liu. Where does that "fundamental disagreement" come from? Does this controversy really occur due to fundamental disagreement?

The difference of view between the U.S. and China can be summarized as a collision between human rights and sovereignty or a controversy between human rights universalism and cultural relativism. China appears to regard Western countries' welcome of Liu's designation as the Nobel Peace Prize winner as an infringement on its sovereignty and cover over its human rights violations in the name of cultural relativism. How much of China's attitude like that will be accepted by the international community in the 21st century, when human rights are regarded as a universal value?

As important concepts in modern society, human rights and sovereignty are often in conflict with each other. In a way, the Charter of the United Nations is self-contradictory, as it stresses the sovereignty of states and their human rights simultaneously. However, the trend in the 1990s and thereafter is that human rights surpass sovereignty. In the case of serious human right violations, other countries' humanitarian interventions are regarded as acceptable. The Chinese government's behavior of calling the international community's criticism about its human rights violations interference in internal affairs is an old-fashioned way of thinking. Its human rights violations can never be justified on the ground of the need to respect a country's sovereignty.

Cultural relativism is the principle that recognizes diversity and holds the belief that a country's culture should be viewed in consideration of its social and cultural characteristics and the flow of history. However, in the modern international society, this human rights-friendly belief has been turned into a concept that separates the Western Hemisphere from the rest of the world. The Western society has often tried to impose Western values on the rest of the world, calling them "universal," and used human rights as a means of applying pressure during negotiations to get a result in their favor. In response, the non-Western society has often defended itself in the name of cultural relativism.

Concerning other countries' pressure for improvement of its human rights situation, China has turned a deaf ear or taken a hardline diplomatic policy. On the back of its ever growing strength, the country could dampen the voices asking for improvement of its human rights situation. However, China will find it hard to get away with it this time, as other countries point fingers at it due to the trade imbalance and the exchange rates of currency as well. The Chinese government should realize that its attitude of limiting people's freedom and suppressing criticisms in the name of cultural relativism will not be tolerated any longer. The concept of cultural relativism was adopted in an effort to pursue universal human rights together rather than to reinforce the state of confrontation between the Western Hemisphere and the rest of the world.

As for the U.S., it is not free from blame concerning its attempt to use the human rights situation of China politically. The world's mass media view the confrontation between the U.S. and China as an exchange rate war spreading to the human rights issue. Perhaps, the U.S. views this incident as a situation favorable to it in connection with its exchange rate war with China. In campaigns for the midterm election scheduled for November 2010, the Republican Party blames the Obama Administration for the economic difficulty, although the current economic crisis was started during the Bush Administration, while the Obama Administration points fingers at China. While it is expected that the odds are in favor of the Republican Party in the midterm election, the Democratic regime will find it a good chance. China's hardline stance against the Western world is a nice target for the Obama Administration's attacks.

The Human Rights norms were not formed by negotiations between countries. Nor is the solution to human rights problems found through confrontation or collision between countries. The human rights issue has emerged as a core concept in an era of "global governance." It is a sector in which diversity, horizontality and self-regulation demanded by global governance are stressed. In other words, the human rights issue is a sector in which norms are formed and problems are settled through the voluntary participation of various actors, such as international organizations, NGOs, and multinationals that form the horizontal network of collaboration. It is a far cry from the past when several world powers made norms and operated the international community vertically.

The human rights issue should maintain its own significance in the process of development. It is not desirable for countries to point fingers at a country concerning its human rights situation. Nor is it right to cover over one's human rights problem in the name of sovereignty. Neither of the following is desirable: the Chinese government's attitude to regard Western countries' response to its human rights situation as interference in internal affairs and U.S. President Barack Obama's pointed remark that China should release Liu Xiaobo. The war of attribution between the two superpowers has an impact on the entire global village. In the era of global governance, countries should not be engaged in struggles over the human rights issue. And the essence of the human rights issue should not be impaired amid ludicrous logic concerning sovereignty or cultural relativism.

---

* JPI PeaceNet No.31 published on November 2, 2010 in Korean

International Development Cooperation and the Role of the Jeju International Training Center (JITC)

RHEE Byung-kook
Korea International Cooperation Agency

The South Korean Government joined the OECD's Development Assistance Committee (DAC) in 2009, played host to the G20 Summit in 2010, and will host the High-Level Forum on Aid Effectiveness (HLF4) in 2011. Thus, the country has succeeded in changing its status from one of the world's poorest countries just fifty years ago to that of an aid donor. It became the first emerging Asian country to host the G20 Summit and take an active part in the work of formulating new aid norms, in addition to playing the role of a coordinator between aid donors and beneficiaries.

The development agenda that should be dealt with by South Korea in its efforts for international development cooperation is becoming more complicated. The world is faced with new challenges such as climate change, international trade, security and human rights, all of which have an impact on development, as well as traditional development agenda items, including poverty, health and education. Developing countries will not be able to achieve growth without addressing these new challenges properly.

Climate change, which results in disasters and affects agriculture and water resources, poses a serious threat to human life in low-income countries. The proliferation of international crime, terrorism and conflicts threaten global human security. Under such circumstances, KOICA, the South Korean Government's grant agency, carries out activities designed to help peace take root in Iraq, Afghanistan, Palestine and Pakistan, and provides support for the East Asia Climate Partnership (EACP) with the focus water management and low-carbon city projects.

In October 2010, the Jeju International Training Center (JITC) was opened as the ninth regional office of the United Nations Institute for Training and Research (UNITAR). Its opening is a matter to be welcomed with open arms, as it will lead to cooperation between the local administrative unit and the international organization. The center is expected to play an important role in enhancing the capabilities of developing countries in the Asia-Pacific region through its policy training programs on peace, the environment and human security for government officials and decision makers in the region, using contents and methods of education developed by UNITAR.

It is noteworthy that the center was established in Jeju Island, as the island is in a geopolitically ideal location for discussion about peace in the Korean Peninsula and Northeast Asia, and has served as the venue for the ROK-USSR (now "Russia") Summit in 1991, the Inter-Korea Peace Festival in 2003, the ROK-Japan Summit in 2004, the biennial Jeju Peace Forum (2001~09), and the ROK-Japan-China Summit in 2010. The island also directly faces problems related to environmental and climate change and is considering pushing ahead with Blue Growth (which refers to an approach to issues relating to climate change and energy from an oceanic prospective) beyond Green Growth, as the part of the country most vulnerable to global warming and as a home to a number of important World Natural Heritage items.

Developing countries will find South Korea's development experience more useful for their purposes than those of more advanced countries. Also, public officials from countries in the Asia-Pacific region can learn from what South Korea experienced in issues relating to the environment and human rights in its promotion of rapid economic and social development. In detail, South Korea will be able to help developing countries make a more realistic approach to such issues as climate change and human security, through the workshops and training programs if offers on a wide range of matters including energy, low-carbon cities, environmental disasters, local economic development, human trafficking, and migrant workers. As for matters pertaining to human security, the country is expected to play a leading role worldwide, as the JITC will be the first of UNITAR's regional training centers to handle them.

As noted in the foregoing, the JITC has certain geopolitical advantages over those training centers in other countries, and can offer an opportunity for those officials from developing countries to learn from the country's experience of seeking development while making efforts to preserve the environment. The country needs to take into account the differences between the systems and policy environments of the beneficiary countries if the JITC's training programs are to be developed more efficiently. Needless to say, the country should provide support for developing countries with the focus on the development of capabilities in broad sectors, helping them to develop their capability to set up their future development plans and encourage their businesses sector and people to adopt changes.

It is expected that the newly launched JTIC will contribute to the development of the capabilities of developing countries in the Asia-Pacific region in the peace, environmental and human security sectors by conducting invigorated and effective activities, and that the beautiful island of Jeju will emerge as an international hub in the relevant sectors.

---

* JPI PeaceNet No.34 published on December 7, 2010 in Korean

China's Human Rights' Actions Speak Louder Than Words?

Max Tsung-Chi YU

National Defense University

Recently, China's best-known dissident Liu Xiaobo was awarded the prestigious Nobel Peace Prize by the Norwegian Nobel Committee for his long and nonviolent struggle for fundamental human rights in China. Although the decision infuriated the Chinese government which responded by calling Liu a criminal and accusing the Nobel Committee of blasphemy to the peace prize, the international community including Taiwan support Liu's nomination, which was a brave choice by the Norwegian Nobel Committee.

The democratic leaders worldwide all support the Nobel Committee's decision and call on Beijing to release Liu Xiaobo, the latest peace prize laureate, as soon as possible. The award is not only a great honor to Liu himself as the first Chinese to receive it but also a great opportunity to show how China can make progress in human rights development. When it comes to be known, the truth will highly inspire admiration from Chinese as it does the international community.

However, the Norwegian Nobel Committee reportedly has made plans for a Peace Prize ceremony on Dec. 10 this year without recipient Liu Xiaobo. China should think thrice before obstructing Liu, his wife and family from receiving the award because it will not lessen the honor in any way. On the contrary, "Liu's absence from the ceremony will confirm the correctness of the Nobel Committee's decision to give him the prize and justify his sacrifice."

The last time no one was present to collect the Nobel Peace Prize was 1935, when the award was given to German socialist Carl Von Ossietzky. In other cases, family representatives were sent to pick up the awards for the missing laureates such as Russian human rights activist Andrei Sakharov in 1975, Poland's Solidarity founder Lech Walesa in 1983, and Burmese opposition leader Aung San Sui Kyi in 1991. It is unwise for China to continue the length of the infamous name list.

Ironically, it was Liu's arrest and imprisonment for initiating Charter 08 that aroused global interest in China's atrocious human rights record and in its wake the firm support for Liu from the international community that is encouraging people in China to fight for freedom.

The reason the Nobel Committee is awarding him the peace prize is to recognize the universality of Liu's call for fundamental freedoms for his people and his advocacy of universal values of human rights in China. Giving the prize to Liu is a form of moral support to the whole human rights movement in China. Particularly, the Norwegian Nobel Committee has long held the view that human rights and peace are closely linked. Human rights are essential for what Alfred Nobel referred to in his will as "fraternity between nations."

In the past decades, Liu has been one of the kingpins in promoting fundamental human rights in China. He was one of the activists in the 1989 Tiananmen Square Student Reform Movement and an eminent drafter of Charter 08, a document calling for increase rule of law, greater respect for human rights, and an end to one-party rule in China.

Last year on 23 Dec. 2009 Liu was sentenced to 11 years in Jinzhou prison, Liaoning province, on charges of "inciting subversion of state power" for his involvement in drafting and circulating Charter 08. Even though compared with any democracy around the world, it was little more than a low-key manifesto for the rights of the Chinese people. Liu has consistently maintained that the sentence violates China's own constitution for citizens' speech and press freedom enshrined in Article 35.

Liu's award need not be a moment of shame or insult for China. This should be a moment of pride, celebrating the fact that one of China's own is recognized as the world's greatest contributor to the advance of human rights and peace. It is hard to believe that Liu is regarded as a criminal in his own country for exercising his right to free speech. In particular, the Chinese government has already signed the International Covenant on Civil and Political Rights and ratified the International Covenant on Economic and Social Rights.

In fact some of China's top leaders have also given similar messages. Deng Xiaoping first mentioned in the 1980s that economic reform could not continue in depth without reformation of the political system in advance. In 2003, Chinese president Hu Jintao reportedly said that the CCP faced inevitable extinction if it did not increase press freedom. More recently, in an interview with CNN, premier Wen Jiabao acknowledged that "Freedom of speech is indispensable … The people's wishes for, and needs for, democracy and freedom are irresistible."

Another Chinese eminent human rights activist Wang Dan also indicates that the Liu Xiaobo effect is greatly encouraging the pro-democracy camp in China. Members of the camp can be traced back all the way up from Peng Tehuai, Liu Shaochi, Hu Yaobang, Zhao Ziyang, Wei Jingsheng, and Hu Jia to all the co-authors of Charter 08. Wang further pointed out that "thanks to the international community's firm support, people in China now have great confidence in their call for democracy and have greater courage to achieve it."

China is seemly facing an international community that is more coherent on the human rights issue as "more and more countries come to the agreement that states cannot insist on absolute sovereignty in their domestic affairs if they abuse the fundamental human rights of their citizens." In other words, if China cannot join together to accomplish this great task, it will sooner or later isolate itself from the international community.

"If China doesn't want to fight a losing battle against the forces of democracy and freedom, China should join the mainstream of civilized humanity by embracing universal values. Such is the only route to becoming a 'great nation' that is capable of playing a positive and responsible role on the world stage." (Keith Richburg)

China has released a human rights action plan following international criticism of its rights record, but its political reformation and human rights action plan cannot always come to a standstill of empty talk; it is time to demonstrate the sincerity to act. Free Liu Xiaobo immediately and end the house arrest imposed on his wife; otherwise, China is making a gross mistake standing on the wrong side of human history.

* JPI PeaceNet No.35 published on December 14, 2010 in English